Student-Led Conferencing Using Showcase Portfolios

Barbara Benson
Susan Barnett

 CORWIN PRESS, INC.
A Sage Publications Company
Thousand Oaks, California

For information address:

Corwin Press, Inc.
A Sage Publications Company
2455 Teller Road
Thousand Oaks, California 91320
E-mail: order@corwinpress.com

SAGE Publications Ltd.
6 Bonhill Street
London EC2A 4PU
United Kingdom

SAGE Publications India Pvt. Ltd.
M-32 Market
Greater Kailash I
New Delhi 110 048 India

Printed in the United States of America

Library of Congress Cataloging-in-Publication Data

Benson, Barbara (Barbara P.)
    Student-led conferencing using showcase portfolios / by Barbara Benson and Susan Barnett.
        p.   cm.
    Includes bibliographical references.
    ISBN 0-8039-6766-7 (pbk.: acid-free paper)
    1. Portfolios in education.   2. Parent-teacher conferences.
I. Barnett, Susan (Susan P.).   II. Title
    LB1029.P67 B46   1998
    371.103—ddc21   98-25475

This book is printed on acid-free paper.

99 00 01 02 03 10 9 8 7 6 5 4 3 2 1

Editorial Assistant: Julia Parnell
Production Editor: Denise Santoyo
Production Assistant: Patricia Zeman
Typesetter/Designer: Janelle LeMaster
Cover Designer: Tracy E. Miller
Cover Photo: Comstock, Inc.

Contents

Foreword

In November 1995, a team of teachers from my school participated in a professional growth opportunity on Portfolios and Student-Led Conferences presented by Barbara Benson and Susan Barnett. The team was looking for a practical and effective answer to a very basic yet perplexing question: What can our school do to improve the quality of student work? Like many teachers, we were frustrated by the "good enough" approach to quality by many of our students who seemed to feel why strive for excellence when mediocrity will do? Barnett and Benson provided a meaningful answer to our question, along with a bonus of classroom-validated materials to help bring a vision into reality.

We knew of the increasing popularity of student portfolios as an alternative assessment instrument, and some of our teachers had even experimented with portfolio assessment. We were also aware of the research that has shown that parent-teacher interviews are greatly enhanced by the participation and even the leadership of the student. It was at that 1995 workshop that Barnett and Benson demonstrated effectively that the marriage of the two key ideas—portfolios and student-led conferences—creates a powerful process that motivates students to self-assess, revise, and take pride in their work. A wider audience of significant people for student work can and does result in high-quality products. Inspired by Barnett and Benson and their ideas, my school has become an Eastern Ontario leader in portfolios and student-led conferences.

It is not surprising that Barnett and Benson and their approach to portfolios and student-led conferencing have been extremely well received by teachers everywhere. All teachers want their students to succeed and to perform and produce at high levels consistently. The authors have traveled extensively throughout the United States and Canada to lead workshops and work directly with teachers in their schools and classrooms. Both have done presentations for the Association for Curriculum Development, the National Staff Development Council, and the National Council of Teachers of English. School districts in California, New York, Texas, North Carolina, and other states and provinces have invited them to help their teachers implement portfolios and student-led conferencing successfully.

All teachers of kindergarten through high school are fortunate that Barnett and Benson decided to produce *Student-Led Conferencing Using Showcase Portfolios,* which is a manual of ideas, strategies, and information developed over many years of teaching and working with teachers. Over the past 5 years, many excellent books about portfolios and student-led conferences have been published, and educators who have read these books will recognize that this manual is based on solid and reliable research about student learning and assessment. *Student-Led Conferencing Using Showcase Portfolios* contributes to the literature in that it provides practical and tested strategies to implement the whole process in a clear, organized, and meaningful way. Teachers and administrators will appreciate the many hours of planning that Barnett and Benson and their many contacts across North America have already done for them and the time that will be saved by using and adapting the strategies in this manual. The authors address each stage of the portfolio and conferencing process—informing all participants, collecting the materials, selecting artifacts to include in the portfolio, reflecting and showcasing the product—through thoughtful and practical ideas.

Our involvement at a workshop by Barbara Benson and Susan Barnett several years ago was a momentous event in my school's quest to motivate students to seek pride in the quality of their work. The use of this manual will offer the same success for any elementary, middle, or high school with the same noble pursuit.

John P. Robson
Head of Social Sciences
Rideau High School
Ottawa-Carleton District Board of Education

Preface

This book is a result of our evolution as teachers and our passion for helping teachers motivate students to learn what is essential to their success beyond school. Like educators across the country, we faced the dilemma of figuring out how to enhance student learning, move toward more authentic assessment of that learning, and report the progress of students more effectively to parents. Our own struggle to do these things led us to two strategies that, in combination, have the power to transform classrooms into the type of learning communities necessary to address some of the largest concerns of American education: student motivation, higher standards for learning, and parent involvement.

Many books are available about portfolios, but none that discusses in detail how to create the portfolios and use them as tools in conferences led by students. A portfolio is an assessment document of student learning, but the conference is the assessment performance that truly demonstrates student learning. Because conferences give the portfolio authenticity, and the portfolio is a necessity in a conference to illustrate the student's learning and progress toward educational goals, it is the marriage of the two strategies that makes a comprehensive assessment. Our book discusses how to implement both. We believe that creating portfolios without the purpose of sharing them with an authentic audience is too much work with too little reward for students and teachers. Perhaps that is why systems that merely collect student portfolios for grades are moving away from using portfolio assessment. Our discussion of portfolios is imbedded in the process for implementing student-led conferences.

By explaining the processes for creating student showcase portfolios to be used in conducting student-led conferences, this book will enable teachers and schools to implement these practices. It is a "cookbook" of recipes for improving student motivation, raising standards of quality in the classroom, and involving parents in the processes of educating their children. It is intended primarily for teachers—both those presently teaching and those learning the profession in teacher training programs. Because the strategies should be a part of any school's ongoing staff development, however, this book is invaluable reading for staff developers, curriculum and instruction directors, building administrators, parents, and school board members in districts involved in school improvement.

We have blended elementary, middle, and high school examples and strategies throughout the book because we feel that the strength of this process is that it is essentially the same at all grade levels and can be the skeleton that aligns portfolio assessment throughout a school system. The processes and strategies in this book are classroom tested. We have used them with our own students, elementary and secondary, and have conducted workshops since 1992 for teachers who have used them successfully in grades K-12. The text includes our experiences as well as those of numerous other educators who have implemented student-led conferencing using showcase portfolios.

Overview   The superstructure on which this book is built is the process of implementing student-led conferencing using showcase portfolios. The order of the chapters follows this process:

- Informing everyone
- Building student portfolios
- Planning and preparing
- Conferencing
- Reflecting and celebrating

Within the chapters, material is organized to answer questions teachers ask most frequently in our workshops.

Chapter 1, "Informing Everyone," explores the theoretical basis for the power of showcase portfolios when they are part of student-led conferences. This chapter connects the processes shared later in the book to sound, research-based rationale on assessment and evaluation of student learning, work, and progress. Then the chapter discusses ways for teachers to inform both parents and students of the process for conferencing and constructing student portfolios.

Chapter 2, "Building Student Portfolios," defines *portfolio* and describes different types of portfolios that may be used to conference. Because we recommend one particular type of portfolio for student-led conferences, we offer numerous suggestions for possible contents for K-12 showcase portfolios in various curriculum areas. The chapter then goes into detailed discussion of the process for creating showcase portfolios in classrooms:

- Collecting necessary work samples
- Selecting what should be included in the portfolios
- Reflecting on the learning these samples represent

Included in this discussion are ways to focus students on quality work and teach them the habit of reflection.

In Chapter 3, "Planning and Preparing Student-Led Conferences," we examine the process for getting ready for student-led conferences. The chapter discusses how to help students prepare and numerous ways to invite and involve parents as well as deal with the logistics of holding conferences in various school configurations. It also includes tips for successful conferences and ideas for giving students credit.

Conducting the actual conferences is discussed in Chapter 4, "Conducting Conferencing." This chapter offers snapshots of conferences at different schools and different grade levels. We give examples of how conferences are conducted in a single classroom as well as in an entire school. This chapter also answers any remaining "Yes, but what if . . . ?" questions teachers and administrators have about implementing student-led conferencing using showcase portfolios.

In Chapter 5, "Reflecting and Celebrating," we discuss ways to have everyone involved reflect on the process with an eye toward improving it next time.

The final chapter, "Improving Student Learning: The Evidence," offers proof of the success of using these combined strategies with students. It also includes the voices of teachers, students, parents, and school administrators as they relate the positive effect that using the strategies has had on them and their schools.

The Resources offer additional help for teachers. Resource A contains sample forms that can be used in the process of creating portfolios and conducting conferences. Resource B discusses other types of portfolios and a related issue, teachers creating their own professional portfolios, which we feel is essential if a teacher is to help students with their showcase portfolios. Finally, the Reference section presents a list of works cited in the text and other sources that offer more information about many of the topics included in the book.

Our purpose in writing this book is to share the methods of implementing two powerful tools for improving student learning so that teachers can use showcase portfolios and student-led conferencing with their students, no matter what grade level or content area they teach. In the effort to improve schools, researchers and theorists have offered educators numerous ideas and programs, but rarely have they given clear and practical processes for turning these theories into practice. These two strategies do just that, and we know that they work—for teachers, for parents, and, most important, for students. Our hope is that this book finds its way into the hands of many teachers who will use it to implement showcase portfolios and student-led conferencing in their classrooms so that these practices become a regular part of how schools do business.

Acknowledgments   As teachers, we have had the good fortune to work with some of the brightest, most knowledgeable, and most dedicated educators in this country. We are eternally grateful for the opportunities that have been given to us to learn and grow as individuals and as facilitators for other's learning. This manual is a result of the collaborative efforts of many people. Significant contributions and suggestions came from the class-rooms of practitioners across the United States and Canada, and we are very grateful for their willingness to try new ideas and to share their knowledge and experiences with us. A sincere thank you goes to those who contributed their ideas, experiences, time, and suggestions to this publication. Of special note, we would like to thank the following people:

- Amy Karbula and Kris Bacca for introducing us to the concept of student-led conferencing
- Susan Kraemer for constant encouragement and support in the process of developing this book
- Dr. Bill Spady and Dr. Kit Marshall for giving us the opportunity to write two earlier manuals on which this current work is based
- John Robson and the teachers of Rideau High School in Ottawa, Ontario, for implementing these strategies in a large secondary school
- Jill Chapman, a kindergarten teacher in Broward County, Florida, for taking our ideas and adapting them to the smallest students
- Sharon Breitenstein, a sixth grade teacher at Valle Crucis Elementary School in Valle Crucis, NC, for being our middle school connection.
- Judy Grissom, principal of East Forsyth High School in Kearnesville, North Carolina, and the teachers in the ninth grade Quality Academy for proving that these strategies help students
- Dianne Porter, principal of Floresville Middle School in Floresville Texas, and the teachers who successfully took these strategies from a special summer school model to their whole school
- Our husbands, Steve and Scott, and sons, Erik, Lincoln, Chris, and Andy, for their understanding, patience, and constant support for our teaching, consulting, and writing
- Our mothers for being exceptional teachers before us and for giving us examples of what caring professional educators should be

About the Authors

Barbara Benson is an international consultant and teacher with more than 20 years of experience in middle school, high school, and university education. She works with school systems in various capacities such as helping to align curriculum, instruction, and assessment practices with higher national and state standards; facilitating the development of performance assessment tasks; and assisting teachers as they apply current theory and research to their classrooms. In December 1996, she and Susan Barnett presented at the National Staff Development Council's annual conference in Vancouver, British Columbia on portfolios and student-led conferencing, and in March 1997, they presented at the Association for Curriculum Development national conference in Baltimore on problem-based learning. She presented two sessions at the 1998 Association for Curriculum Development national conference on a successful model for school improvement and aligning school practice with new standards and assessments. She has published numerous articles on classroom practice and has written a manual for secondary teachers on portfolios and student-led conferencing. Presently, she is working extensively with schools and systems in New York, Texas, and North Carolina, as well as supervising student teachers for Appalachian State University in Boone, North Carolina.

Susan Barnett is a teacher with the Watauga County Schools in North Carolina. She has been in the field of education for 25 years. Her work experience includes teaching grades K-4. For the past 5 years, she has worked as an educational consultant with school systems across the United States and Canada. During the 1995-96 school year, for example, she was an on-site consultant with the Los Angeles School District in its school reform efforts. She is also the author of several articles about innovative teaching strategies, and she wrote a teacher's manual on implementing student portfolios in elementary classrooms. She and Barbara Benson were awarded state recognition for their Ed Loop program, a literacy intervention model. She is presently working with low-performing schools as an Assistance Team Reviewer for the North Carolina Department of Public Instruction.

CORWIN
PRESS

The Corwin Press Logo—a raven stiding across an open book—represents the happy union of courage and learning. We are a professional-level publisher of books and journals for K-12 educators, and we are committed to creating and providing resources that embody these qualities. Corwin's motto is "Success for All Learners."

Informing Everyone 1

Informing everyone involved in the creation of student portfolios and the conducting of student-led conferences is crucial to the eventual success of the undertaking. Before teachers can determine how they want to go about informing students, parents, and administrators about their plans, however, they need to understand these two strategies and know the theoretical basis for their power as educational tools. With a knowledge of the reasons why these two strategies work together to help students learn, a teacher is better prepared to explain to everyone concerned why he or she is using them. The teacher is also better able to adjust and improve the process when necessary so that it will work with all students in his or her unique classroom. Therefore, before we give ideas for how to involve students and parents in the process, we want to inform teachers about the "what" and "why" of student-led conferencing using showcase portfolios.

What Is Student-Led Conferencing?

Student-led conferencing is simply having students conduct formal conferences with their parents or guests to display their schoolwork as well as discuss their learning, educational goals, and strategies for meeting those goals. Such conferences are a continuation of the classroom conversations about learning that take place between the teacher and the students throughout the development of a portfolio. They offer the authentic outside audience that is necessary for portfolios to be serious, real-world tasks, and they bring parents into the assessment process.

The inclusion of parents in school assessments of learning is one of the standards for assessment of reading and writing developed by the International Reading Association (IRA) and the National Council of Teachers of English (NCTE). In their rationale for this standard, the IRA and the NCTE (1994) assert that "in many schools, parents stand on the periphery of the school community, some feeling hopeless, helpless, and unwanted. Parents must become active participants in the assessment process" (p. 37). Involving parents in the assessment process "includes the use of communication and reporting procedures between school and home that enable parents to talk in productive ways with their children" about their learning (p. 38). Student-led conferences can be this type of parent-student communication.

All teachers realize that parental support is crucial if students are to succeed in school, and any effort we can expend to enhance that parent support will benefit all participants in the educational process. Student-led conferences are a relatively easy way to inform parents of student performance and encourage the home support the students need to improve and continue learning.

In addition to bringing parents into the school experience of the students in a positive way, student-led conferencing helps students develop skills necessary to be successful in the future. The process of preparing for and conducting conferences allows students to look at their own performances in the classroom, set goals and strategies for improving future work, organize a presentation about their learning, carry out that presentation, and reflect on its effectiveness with the goal of improving future performances. For older students, this process is similar to interviews for college entrance, scholarships, and jobs and to job performance review conferences with work supervisors. Students and parents must be shown the similarities between school conferences and future situations students will face. Parents will then see that they are helping their children practice for some crucial adult performances, and the students themselves will have additional motivation for performing well. The authentic nature of student-led conferencing provides younger students with a relevant, real-world context and application for their learning. As an authentic task, student-led conferencing has the power to motivate students to do high-quality work and the added benefit of eliciting parent support for the student, teacher, and the school.

Why Do Student-Led Conferences Using Showcase Portfolios Work?

Portfolios and student-led conferences are so powerful in the classroom because they are applications of the theories involved in the educational research on the use of authentic tasks and assessment as tools to enhance student motivation and learning. Authentic tasks are real-world activities that people perform in the seven spheres of their lives:

- Personal potential and wellness
- Learning
- Meaningful and fulfilling pursuits
- Physical and cultural environment
- Group and community memberships
- Work and productive endeavors
- Close and significant relationships (Spady, 1994)

Such authentic learning is often inspired by the use of real problems that require critical thinking and complex problem solving. Creating a portfolio and conducting a conference with parents are two authentic tasks that involve students in multiple problem-solving situations and can encourage as well as teach critical thinking skills.

What Do You Mean by *Authentic*?

Portfolios are authentic because they are used by adults to pursue professional and personal goals. Artists, models, architects, advertising agents, and even the kitchen specialist at the local hardware store have portfolios to illustrate their best work to future employers and clients. Educators studying for certification as principals are being asked to compile portfolios in progressive programs such as the one at Indiana University of Pennsylvania (Willis, 1994). Teachers and student teachers are also being asked to develop portfolios as part of their evaluations. Whether or not a portfolio is being required in the system, a teacher who is planning to implement portfolios in the classroom really needs to begin a professional portfolio as students are beginning their learning portfolios (see Resource B). If the teacher is developing a portfolio as students are doing so, the teacher will have a much better grasp of the process, problems, and rewards of the activity and therefore be able to model and facilitate the student process. Portfolios are real documents in the adult world, and creating them can help students connect classroom activities to the world beyond school.

Creating portfolios for a grade only does not make them authentic. All adult professional portfolios are meant to be shared with someone for the purpose of showing what the portfolio creator can do. Student portfolios become authentic when they are intended to be used beyond the classroom. Student portfolios created for a class can be used to apply for jobs, to gain admission to college, to validate exemption from college classes, or to qualify for scholarships. Universities such as Miami University of Ohio are aiding in this process by having students use writing portfolios compiled during their senior year of high school as a way to test out of the introductory writing course at the university ("College Placement Portfolios Help High Schools Teach Writing," 1993, p. 7). These previous real-world uses are, however, available only to secondary students who are close to graduating. What can help make creating a student portfolio real for elementary and middle school students?

Currently, most student portfolios at all levels are still used only as a form of test to be handed in to the teacher or system. When this happens, students do not own the document and are no more motivated to do well on the portfolio than they are on any school evaluation. Teachers have discovered that in cases like this, students just give them the same quality work they would have turned in before, but now they have collected all the "stuff" into a pile!

Bringing parents into the picture to view the portfolios in student-led conferences, however, automatically makes portfolios authentic for all students. As one 16-year-old stated, "Explaining my work to my father by showing my portfolio is the most authentic assessment possible!" The real value of portfolios as documents of authentic learning and quality work is in the fact that they can, when shared with an audience beyond the classroom, motivate students to do a better job than they might ordinarily have done. Like all of us, students are motivated by the relevance and significance of the tasks they are asked to do. A real-world task such as discussing learning and progress with a significant adult is naturally motivating and challenging for students. If we want to do something about the apathy that prevents learning in many classrooms, we should heed this connection between motivation and authentic student tasks. As W. Edwards Deming observed, "Intrinsic motivation is the engine for improvement. If it is kept alive and nourished, quality can and will occur. If it is killed, quality dies with it" (cited in Aguayo, 1990, p. 103).

Authentic tasks such as student-led conferences using showcase portfolios can improve student motivation for class work and, therefore, raise the quality of that work—two goals all teachers have for their students! Not only do portfolios and student-led conferences allow for authentic work in the classroom, they also allow for more authentic assessment and reporting of that work.

What Is an *Authentic Assessment*?

The term *assessment* is being used in education for everything, and the word *authentic* tends to be attached if a particular test is not traditional pen and paper. Current use of these two terms is often in error, however, because much of what is called assessment and authentic is neither. *Authentic assessment* is a term appropriate only for times when student learning is applied in a complex, real-world situation, and assessment is more than an event for a grade—it is a complex and long-term process.

The root word, *assess,* means to sit beside. In other words, an assessment should be a mentoring process through which teachers sit with students, and together they look at where the student work falls in relation to set criteria to make plans for the next steps in reaching or exceeding the criteria. Assessment is an ongoing dialogue between the student and teacher, not a singular event. This is far from the present state assessments that occur on a set date and do not get results back to teachers until the students have finished the school year. In these situations, there is no real ongoing conversation between the teacher and student based on the information they may have gotten from the test event. The difference between an assessment and a test, as one high school student explained very vividly, is that if assessment is "sit beside," then a test is "stand over."

A test is an evaluation intended to give information about how a student is doing at a certain checkpoint. As much as we would prefer to do assessment, we must also evaluate student learning because there are many people who need to know how students are doing. Portfolios can be used to gain information for assessment and evaluation, but teachers need to be clear about which they are doing at a given time. The assessment should be happening all along the way as students and teachers are working together. Evaluation should happen at the end of the process to report student learning and progress toward goals and expectations.

In carrying out the process of authentic assessment, teachers should ask four questions:

1. How are you doing now?
2. What do you need to work on to improve?
3. What strategies could you use to improve?
4. What have you learned, and how can you use it beyond the classroom?

These four questions demonstrate the process that all of us go through in learning situations. We take stock of what we know, we decide what we need to know or do next to improve our performance, we plan strategies to improve, and we decide how we will use the information or skills we have acquired. If a written test is the only evaluation of student learning, the process of assessment never formally goes beyond the first question. Only students who are already motivated because they see some relevance to the learning activities in the class will ever go on to questions 2 through 4. Most of our students are not able to apply this process to our classes. Consequently, we must help them internalize this process by practicing it through the way we assess their learning.

Portfolios, which are developed over a period of time and involve student self-assessment, and student-led conferences have the potential to become authentic assessments that can encourage and teach the processes needed for students to carry the learning in the classroom far beyond the classroom into their adult lives. An additional assessment advantage to student-led conferencing is that it actively involves the parents or guests of the student in the process of assessment. In a student-led conference, the parents are sitting beside their child and discussing the learning demonstrated in the portfolio and the child's goals and plans for improvement.

The use of portfolios and student-led conferences can not only improve student motivation, improve student learning, and change assessment practices but can also change teaching methods and, consequently, the whole learning environment in the classroom and school. In compiling a portfolio and preparing for a parent conference, the students are the ones doing the actual work.

They are beginning to take ownership of and responsibility for their learning, while the teacher plays the roles of guide and facilitator—roles educational reformers are encouraging teachers to assume. These roles insist that teachers help students discover the relevance of their learning, solve their individual learning problems, make personal decisions about their work, and develop the communication skills needed to discuss their learning. A classroom where students take such an active part in the work going on will be a different classroom from the one where the teacher is the giver of knowledge to passive students seated in neat rows of desks. As Barbara Barbour, a math teacher in Vermont, said, "Using portfolios has changed my approach to teaching math, and it has changed the way students learn. They're doing more creative work by problem solving, and they're excited by the process" (cited in Merina, 1993, p. 5). Portfolios used in student-led conferences move students and teachers toward more authentic work, learning, assessment, and, inevitably, instruction.

Such movement demonstrates the five standards of authentic instruction proposed by Fred M. Newmann and Gary G. Wehlage (1993) because they require

1. Higher-order thinking
2. Depth of knowledge
3. Connectedness to the world beyond the classroom
4. Substantive conversation—student and teacher talking within the classroom to learn and understand the substance of a subject
5. Social support for student achievement

Portfolios and student-led conferences demand higher-order thinking and depth of knowledge because students have to organize, make decisions, explain and justify those decisions, and convey their content learning to an audience beyond the classroom. The conversations that take place between teacher and student, student and student, and student and parent offer social support for student achievement and help teachers be more effective in teaching content and encouraging students to use their minds well.

How Do I Start With Students?

Getting started is always the hardest part. As Dana Sheedy (personal communication, March 3, 1998), first- and second-grade teacher at Batesville School in Uvalde, Texas, says, "The most difficult part was getting started. I wanted to do this last year, but never knew how to do it. This year, I decided to just jump in and do it!" This is exactly how it feels when you first try student-led conferencing. Because it is so different from the way we have been trained as teachers, it often feels very "messy."

It's as if you are jumping off a cliff in to an unknown, arms flailing and legs kicking; but don't worry, the excitement students get from having some control and say over their own learning will carry you through the rough patches. You have to have the faith that it will work. Even when we did not feel that we were really as prepared as we needed to be when parents and guests showed up for conferences, all went well. Our best advice for getting started is to get a friend, hold hands, take a deep breath, and jump off that cliff. We promise, you both will fly!!

Once you have made the decision to begin and have determined some of the logistics for creating the portfolios and organizing for conferences (see Chapters 2 and 3), you need to inform students. Student preparation, elementary through high school, begins the first day of school, when students are told conferences will be part of the school year. Students need to be informed about the reasons for conducting the conferences and the benefits of taking part. Some of the benefits are:

• For younger students, a chance to "brag" about and share good work, some uninterrupted time with mom and/or dad, an opportunity to practice communication and reading skills, and a chance to share school experiences

• For middle school students, an opportunity to demonstrate growing maturity, a chance to talk to parents in an organized, formal, and nonconfrontational way, and a forum to share the range of their school activities and growing competence in content areas

• For high school students, a practice for future job, college, and scholarship interviews, an audience for their increasingly complex knowledge and skills in content areas, and a chance to visit with parents whom they may not see very much due to their own activities and job commitments

Although younger students are very willing and excited about conferencing with their parents, middle school and high school students often approach this idea with mixed emotions. Because teenagers are trying to be adults, free of parental control, they may balk at the idea of leading a parent conference at first. They will, however, like the opportunity to please their parents by showing what they are learning and can do. In preparing high school students for conferences, one teacher led them in a mantra to remind them of why they were having conferences and to get them "psyched" for the experience. They would chant, "We are doing this to prove that we are mature, organized, intelligent, and responsible adults!" It always worked, and students went into their conferences convinced of the value of holding them as well as their ability to do them well. Regardless of the age of students, they will all be anxious about whether or not they can conduct such a conference, so they will need to be assured from the beginning that class activities will prepare them to do a great job when the conferences roll around.

It always helps to be able to show students what portfolios and conferencing looks like as you inform them, but it is not necessary. The first year a teacher has students create portfolios and conduct conferences, it is usually impossible to have models of student portfolios to show or veterans of conferences to share their experiences with a class. If a teacher has never seen a student portfolio, when students ask what a portfolio looks like, it is OK to answer that the class will figure it out together. The uncertainty of that may make some students and teachers uncomfortable, but it does have one advantage. It involves the students in the process from the beginning and demonstrates to them that learning is not something they alone are expected to do. Teachers have to try new things and learn as well! If what we are modeling for students is lifelong learning, it is good for students to see that we do not always have the answers for every question or the patterns of how something must be done. The greatest learning experiences are the ones where the door is open, where we do not have all the answers.

Who Are You, and Why Are You Here?

The process of informing students and getting them started also involves setting an initial benchmark by which student progress can be measured throughout the year. Students need to know where they are starting in order to set goals and be able to talk about their own progress when conferencing time arrives. Therefore, after students have been told they will be leading a conference with their parents where they will use a portfolio as evidence of their learning, they need to make an opening statement about who they are and what they hope to gain during the year's schooling. We always ask our students to answer two questions— who are you and why are you here?—at the beginning of school. Even the youngest students can introduce themselves with a self-portrait or a scripted answer to the questions. With really young children, there may only be the self-portrait, but this can be the basis for seeing development in the child's perceptions of the world, fine motor skills, and reading readiness. Older students can write reflective pieces or an essay to complete this assignment. The second question is very important for students to consider because it can lead to goal setting for the year or for the first marking period.

Having students set some goals for themselves is part of the first stage of the conferencing process. They should set no more than three goals, and they should also list a strategy to help them achieve each goal. Students often do not know what is meant by "strategy." In fact, many students who struggle in school don't even know that there are strategies for learning. It has been a mystery of the universe for them, something that some students were born knowing how to do! Therefore, the teacher will need to discuss what "strategy" means. For example, if a student's goal is to improve test scores, simply studying harder might not be an appropriate or specific enough strategy. This would be particularly true if that student has lost the textbook the class is using and never does the reading. Perhaps finding the book is the first strategy that needs to be employed!

Once students have drawn or written their beginning statement, goals, and the strategies they plan to use to reach goals, these pieces should be collected by the teacher. Because discussions of progress throughout the year will be anchored on these documents, they need to be saved for use later. Students will not realize the significance of these papers to the process of the upcoming conferences and may not be able to find them later when they are needed. After these papers are safely collected, students are ready to begin their year of learning.

How Do I Inform Parents?

Just like the students, parents need to know about the upcoming conference plans and specific dates as soon in the year as possible. They also need to know the rationale behind the conference and the logistics for participating. An excellent time to introduce parents to the concepts of portfolios and conferencing is at the first parent meeting or open house of the school year. In schools where portfolios and student-led conferencing will be a schoolwide activity, the fall open house can be planned specifically for this purpose. But if the open house comes after the first month of school or will offer the teacher only a few minutes with parents, the best way to inform parents is to invite them to an orientation meeting early in the school year. In such a meeting, the teacher would:

• Explain that the conference will be a time of sharing and celebration of the work done during the grading period, and that the child will be in charge of the conference

• Describe the process to be used in preparing for the conference, developing the portfolios, and completing the conference

• If possible, tell parents the date of the first conference so that they can get it on their calendars

• Let parents know they should allow 20 minutes for the conferences (Most conferences actually last longer than the allotted time because the parents are interested and the conversation goes beyond the specific items the students prepare to share.)

- Explain that parents can schedule separate teacher-parent conferences to deal with specific problems if desired or needed

- Share the purposes and powerful benefits of student-led conferencing, for example, student-led conferences provide students with the opportunity

  - To become responsible for their own work
  - To learn organizational skills
  - To be involved in the assessment of their learning
  - To improve their communication skills
  - To include their parents in their learning experiences
  - To learn to set and achieve realistic goals

- Emphasize how parents can support their child by attending the conference (their participation allows the students to practice real-world skills with a supportive audience who has the child's best interest at heart)

- Explain that parents will be asked to help document the conference with a reflection

- Answer questions and address parent concerns

The teacher should also provide a parent handout with the main points of the presentation and details of the dates, times, and places of the upcoming conferences.

The teacher should invite administrators to this meeting because their support will be important in the success of the conferences. Their presence at the meeting also signals to parents that these conferences are an approved activity.

Jay McTighe (1997) offers an analogy that is a clear way of explaining to parents what a portfolio is: "If a test or a quiz represents a snapshot (a picture of learning at a specific moment) then a portfolio is more like a photo album—a collection of pictures showing growth over time" (p. 12). Parents understand that a photo album of their child's year would be much richer than one or two pictures. They will be delighted to know that they will be receiving such a collection at the end of the school year.

Parents, especially of elementary students, need to understand that implementing portfolios in a classroom changes some of the normal practices that parents associate with school. One thing that differs from traditional practice is that students will not be bringing home great quantities of completed schoolwork on a daily or even weekly basis. The teacher needs to explain to parents that student work must remain in the classroom so that students can have work to select from when assembling their portfolios. Initially, this may concern some parents who use the daily work their children bring home to follow their children's school progress. During the first parent meeting, the teacher needs to assure parents that teacher-parent communication will be accomplished through weekly newsletters, notes, student-parent letters, and other alternative communication methods, including student-led conferencing.

Because student-led conferencing differs from traditional parent-teacher conferences, parents often fear that unless they meet with their child's teacher, they will not know what is going on at school. As teachers inform parents about student-led conferencing, they need to stress that although the child is in charge of the conference, parents will have a better understanding of their child's strengths and weaknesses by hearing from their child firsthand and by seeing work in the portfolio. Parents also need to know that they can request a conference with the teacher at another time if necessary.

Prior to the parent meeting, the teacher may want to ask someone to videotape the meeting. The videotape can then be copied and made available for parents who are unable to attend. These videotapes will enable the teacher to be consistent with information that he or she shares with parents and are invaluable tools to inform parents of new students who join the class later in the school year.

Parents can also be informed with a letter home, but this is not as effective as discussion at a meeting. If a letter is sent, it needs to go out before collecting artifacts for the portfolio begins. To ensure that parents get such a letter, it is best to have students get these signed and returned to the teacher for filing (see Boxes 1.1 and 1.2).

Because showcase portfolios and student-led conferencing may be totally new concepts to parents, they need to be informed early and kept abreast of the process throughout the year. Chances are there is not one method that will suffice to reach all parents, so teachers and schools will have to try many ways to ensure parental knowledge, understanding, and support of the process. Having students and parents understand why they are taking part in the process is essential to making the conferencing experience beneficial to all. Therefore, teachers must inform, educate, and involve students and parents in the process again and again during the year. By the way, once parents attend their first student-led conference with their child, they will understand and support the effort 100%!

Box 1.1. Sample Letter for Elementary School Parents

Dear Parents,

This year your child will be keeping a portfolio. The portfolio supplements the report card and is a way for students, parents, and teachers to see a child's progress throughout the year.

Just as artists, investment brokers, lawyers, and other professionals use portfolios to showcase their best work, your child will use the portfolio to showcase his or her best schoolwork. With my assistance, every child will choose work samples to place in the portfolio as the year progresses. These samples will come from all areas of the curriculum. Students will also include work samples that they think are special. Because the children will need to keep samples through the year, we will not be sending home daily work. All student work will be kept in a works in progress (WIP) folder in the classroom. You are welcome to come and look through your child's WIP folder at any time. The students and I will keep you informed of what is happening in the classroom with a weekly letter.

This year, the students will be learning how to evaluate their own work and how to set goals for future growth. Together, your child and I will meet on a regular basis and discuss these evaluations and goals. Part of the student-led conference will be to share students' own evaluations of their work as well as their goals for improvement with you. Your child will bring his or her portfolio home at the end of the school year.

If you have any questions about the portfolios we will be keeping, I will be happy to answer them. Please call me at 555-1212.

Sincerely,

Ms. Barnett

Box 1.2. Sample Letter for Secondary School Parents

Dear Parents,

As the new school year begins, I want to welcome you to our 180-day adventure in learning. This year we will be doing a number of things differently in an effort to improve the learning that takes place and the quality of the work that students produce. I am very excited about the opportunity to work with you and your child.

Attached you will find a syllabus for the year that gives an overview of the content and procedures we will follow. Please sign and return the Signature Page that follows to indicate that you have read the material.

Two major additions to the year's work will be student portfolios and student-led conferences. A week before the end of the first and third marking periods, we will be having student-led parent conferences to keep you informed of your child's progress in the course. Your child will conduct the conference using a showcase portfolio to document course work and learning progress. The portfolio will be a collection of the student's best work, and no work will go into the portfolio until it meets quality standards at an excellent or acceptable level. Students will be given the information, practice, and help necessary to get their work to an acceptable level, but they must take advantage of these opportunities by attending class regularly and keeping up with assignments. When needed, I will also offer extra help and work time before and after school. Because research clearly shows that parental involvement and support are important to a student's success, I sincerely hope that you will support my efforts to provide the best possible learning experience for students by encouraging your son or daughter to take responsibility for his or her learning and by attending the conferences.

On the evenings of August 31 and September 2, I will be having parent information meetings to discuss the student portfolios and student-led conferencing. The meetings will begin at 7:00 p.m. in the lower part of the high school library. I hope you will be able to attend one of these meetings. If you have any questions or wish to talk to me about the upcoming year, please use the Comments portion of the attached Signature Page to respond or request an appointment. I will be in touch with you as quickly as possible. I am looking forward to getting to know your son or daughter as the year progresses, and hope to see you on the evening of August 31 or September 2.

Sincerely,

Ms. Benson

2 Building Student Portfolios

What Is a Portfolio?

The term *portfolio* has been in wide use in educational circles in recent years, and there are many definitions of the word. The original definition, according to *Webster's Seventh New Collegiate Dictionary,* is "a portable case for carrying papers or drawings" (p. 662) This definition brings to mind the artist with a large cardboard cover for his or her works. As the term is being used in schools, however, it usually refers to a collection of a student's work with emphasis on what the student can do rather than on student mistakes, but views vary on what should be included in a portfolio and how the portfolio should be used. The two definitions that we prefer and have used in designing portfolios for our classes are

- A portfolio is a "collection of examples of a student's work which may be used for evaluation, information, and celebration" (North Carolina Department of Public Instruction, 1992).
- A portfolio is "a record of learning that focuses on students' work and their reflections on the work" (Seidel & Walters, 1992).

One of these definitions clarifies the uses we make of student portfolios, and the other speaks to the need for student reflection to accompany work a student chooses for the collection. Together, these two definitions are an effective guideline for teachers, schools, and systems planning to use portfolios (see p. 106 in Resource A).

The portfolio itself—the container for the student work—can be any number of things. In the early elementary grades, teachers have found that colored folders work best for student portfolios. Each student receives a colored folder with his or her name on the front. Some teachers also have their students personalize the front of the folders with artwork. Different colored folders are designed for each marking period. For example, red is for the first 9 weeks, yellow is for the second 9 weeks, green is for the third, and blue is for the fourth. Each marking period, a new folder and its contents are placed in the larger, official, laminated portfolio folder. Eventually, all the folders are included in the portfolio folder, becoming a complete student portfolio for the school year.

In many intermediate grades, middle school, high school, and college classes, a 3-ringed binder is most often used because of its professional appearance and adaptability to the type of work secondary and postsecondary students tend to do. Separators may be used to separate samples into various classes, subjects, or marking periods. The portfolio binders can be stored in crates, on shelves, or in a filing cabinet.

In addition to folders and binders, teachers could use boxes, accordion envelopes like artists and musicians use, baskets, colorful plastic crates, or any other type of container that fits the nature of the work being collected. Often teachers want to include audio- and videotapes with the student portfolios in addition to other material that is not standard 8″ × 11″. To help little ones (kindergarten through third grade) keep their "stuff" together, teachers can put the student portfolio and tapes in clean, unused pizza boxes donated by a local pizza parlor. The pizza boxes stack neatly on any shelf in the classroom and keep the contents safe, secure, and manageable for youngsters. This type of container has also been used in middle schools, where one boy reports that it is great because it makes all his stuff smell like pizza!

Some schools with high-tech capabilities are using electronic portfolios where the "container" is a disk or CD-ROM. This storage method solves the space problem of keeping 20 to 150 portfolio containers in a classroom and is most likely the way student work will be stored in the future. As David Niguidula (1997) reports,

> For the past few years, a team at the Annenberg Institute for School Reform and the Coalition of Essential Schools, with support of IBM, has been investigating one such technology—the digital portfolio. Digital portfolio software is used to create a multimedia collection of student work and connect that work to performance standards. (p. 26)

As long as the basic elements are included in the portfolio design, the possibilities for the portfolio container itself are limitless. The deciding factor for both the container and the contents of the portfolio should be who will be using the portfolio and for what reason.

Although we advocate using showcase portfolios for student-led conferencing, many types of portfolios can be used in a classroom. Sometimes using one type is either required or a good way to begin the process of keeping student portfolios and having conferences with students about their work. With that in mind, we include discussions of other types of portfolios in Resource B.

We believe teachers must decide what type of portfolio will be most useful with a particular class, setting, or curriculum. The type of portfolio should suit the purposes of that portfolio, and those purposes can be determined by answering a few key questions:

1. Why is student work being kept?
2. Who will be looking at the work?
3. What information will the audience be looking for in the portfolio?

Once these questions are answered, it is easier to select the format, or combination of formats, that will best serve the purpose and conditions for developing the portfolios.

What Is a Showcase Portfolio?

Showcase portfolios are ones like professionals use to display their best work. In a student showcase portfolio, only the best representative pieces from a given period of time are included. An analogy for a showcase portfolio is a published collection of a writer's best work. The writer has the opportunity to revise and improve pieces after the editor reads and comments on them because the goal is to have the best possible versions in the published book. Another analogy is a model's photograph portfolio. No high-fashion model selects the "fat" pictures to be included, only the ones that make her look slim and elegant. As applied to the classroom, the student has the opportunity to select and rework evaluated, representative class assignments to create a high-quality portfolio. Using a showcase portfolio, a teacher can demand higher-quality work from all students in their finished portfolios, and students can meet the requirements because they are given expanded opportunities to learn and demonstrate their knowledge and skills.

In the classroom that requires quality work and has established standards in place, students will strive for quality and want their portfolios to reflect their excellent work. Unfortunately, quality takes time, and time is the nemesis of most teachers. The payoff for teachers who allow the time needed is that in providing students with expanded opportunities to rework poor quality pieces before they go into the portfolio, teachers help motivate student to complete class work, provide one last chance to finish a class assignment, reinforce quality standards, and improve student success.

In our classrooms, we have found that showcase portfolios motivate students to do their best work. Such portfolios are personal and authentic. Students get to show off what they can do in this format; therefore, they give their best. Students also know that adults in the world beyond school have and use showcase portfolios in their professional lives. This fact makes these portfolios particularly relevant and adaptable to the needs of students, even after high school graduation. The motivation inherent in doing an "adult" portfolio, combined with the real audience that will look at it in the student-led conference, leads to students working harder and producing higher-quality results.

Ideas for showcase portfolios:

- Have students examine some professional portfolios so that they can determine what components make up a portfolio. Have them discuss the elements that make a portfolio look professional and complete. If possible, invite a professional to talk to students about the use and development of his or her portfolio.

- If the teacher has or is working on a professional portfolio, it is wonderful to share this with the students. If students see the teacher in the process of developing a portfolio, it gives authenticity to their own process and portfolio work.

- Evaluate student work when it is first done, return it to students for correction, and have students file it in a works in progress folder. At the end of a grading period, have students select pieces from the works in progress folder and prepare them for the portfolio. This preparation might include rewriting, revising, correcting, or writing an assessment of the piece that includes an explanation of the errors with corrections and perhaps additional student-designed examples of the concepts to illustrate that the student did eventually learn the material.

- Provide models of student work to assist students in producing quality work. As students complete tasks, closely monitor their work and provide feedback on the type of quality work they need to be doing. By having students make "on the spot" corrections before filing their work in their works in progress folder, much of the student work will be ready for the showcase portfolio, thus saving a lot of time later in the final development stages of the portfolio process.

- Pre- and post-tests along with a commentary can become another form of documentation of learning for the portfolio. Prior to beginning a new unit, have students take a pretest on the new material. Following the pretest, have students analyze and reflect on their performance. This process not only saves valuable teaching time for the teacher by determining what students know and don't know, it also encourages students to set goals for their own learning. Once the material has been taught, students take the same test again and compare their pre- and posttest results.

- For other tests, students could be asked to take retests on material they initially did not understand. They may not need to take a retest of every poor grade, however. Sometimes a written correction of the test with some form of written test assessment where the student explains what he or she did well on the test, what he or she did not do well and why, what he or she would need to do in the future to improve test scores, and a strategy he or she could use for improving on the next test is more useful than a retest.

- A showcase portfolio can easily be adapted to any course in school and serve real purposes in the world beyond. It can hold work from all classes a student might be taking that year, and can include job- or college-related pieces such as a résumé, generic recommendation letters from teachers, acceptance letters from postsecondary schools, and scholarship awards. Many secondary schools are using such portfolios in their school-to-work efforts to help students make the transition to the work world.

- Showcase portfolios can be organized chronologically so that there are sections for each marking period, or they can be organized by type of assignment, with the first marking period's homework, for example, in the back of the homework section and the latest grading period's homework samples added to the front.

- Showcase portfolios can show a student's progress as well as best work. If the best from each marking period is included, progress should be evident in the artifacts from different parts of the year. Students should also be asked to comment on evident progress in their reflections.

- If there is a concern that the showcase portfolio will give parents a false sense of the child's abilities since everything included will be quality work, the child should have the works in progress folder to show parents as well. In this way, parents will see that a lot of work went into the finished pieces in the portfolio and that the student did other work as well as what is collected in the showcase. This larger view of the child's work should give the parents a better perspective on their child's progress.

What Goes in a Showcase Portfolio?

The contents of a student portfolio should be determined by the work the student is doing, what the portfolio is intended to demonstrate, and who will be looking at the portfolio and for what reason. A showcase portfolio should contain representative samples of whatever significant work is required in the class and student reflections or commentaries on that work and the learning that is occurring. A teacher must look at the required curriculum and skills for the course, the lessons planned for a particular grading period, and the types of assignments students will be doing to plan what might be in the portfolios. For the teacher planning to use student portfolios, the question is simply, What work are students doing in my class, and how can they illustrate it in their portfolios?

Possible Showcase Portfolio
Artifacts for Various Content Areas

The Arts

- Samples or photos of visual creations
- Audio- or videotapes of performances
- Samples of playbills, musical programs, or gallery viewing notes
- Reviews in school and community newspapers of performances or gallery exhibits
- Samples of audience responses to performances or gallery exhibits
- Scripts or scores used in performances with notes by the individual student concerning his or her part in the production
- Audio- or videotapes of auditions for plays or chairs in musical groups
- Audiotapes of individual students playing an instrument or singing (these could be made several times during a school year to show student progress in the field)
- Sketches and models of artwork that show the development of a completed piece or the artist's method of working
- Original musical compositions—both in written form and in performance
- Research projects where students investigate famous artists, musicians, and performers
- Student-authored critiques of performances or gallery exhibits the student attended
- Journal entries on field trips to view art, watch a play, or attend a musical performance
- Interviews with professionals in the arts
- Awards and certificates for performances and attendance at specific clinics, competitions, camps, and institutes

English, Language Arts, and Communications

- Samples of different types of writing: creative and expository
- A student-selected, satisfying, high-quality piece (Seidel & Walters, 1992)
- A student-selected, less-than-satisfying piece (Seidel & Walters, 1992)
- "Free picks" selected by the student and teacher (Seidel & Walters, 1992)

- Student logs or journal entries that provide a picture of the student's development of insight and working process (Seidel & Walters, 1992)
- Evidence of connections between the works read in class and the world beyond: reviews and reactions to current events, television, movies, dramas, and speeches
- Evidence of student use beyond the classroom of the writing process being learned in class
- A "biography of a work" that includes all prewriting notes, drafts, revisions, and reflections that contributed to the completion of the project (Seidel & Walters, 1992)
- Samples of homework, class work, group assignments, essays, tests, projects, letters, and research
- Pictures or videos of the student working in class, presenting to the class, or showing finished projects
- Annotated bibliography of reading done outside of class
- For younger students: story maps; storyboards (sequence of events); puppets; posters; collages; book jackets; diary of a character; critiques of reading; stories; newspaper articles; comic strips; summaries; flap books with a beginning, middle, and end; illustrations; shape books; advertisements; author studies; letters; bookmarks; selected journal pages; self-reflections; cooperative writing; letters; reports; research; recipes; poetry; cartoons; interviews; surveys; letters; lists; graphic organizers; rewriting a story with a new ending, a new situation, a new chapter, or an epilogue; directions for a game; home and class books

Foreign Languages

- Writing samples such as rewrites of assigned pieces or examination essays
- Self-assessment sheets identifying and discussing the best work during a marking period in each of the four language skill areas (listening, speaking, reading, and writing) and the areas that the student needs to work on improving in the next marking period
- Explanation of a risk the student took in learning the language and examples of how the student is using the language beyond the classroom
- Outlines and reactions to television programs in the target language
- Summaries and reactions to music videos produced in the target language
- Reviews of plays or films produced in the target language

- Videos or audiotapes of students speaking the target language, making class presentations in the target language, interviewing someone in the target language, or performing plays, skits, or music in the target language
- Summaries and reviews of articles read from the World Wide Web, foreign language magazines, or newspapers (photocopies of the articles should accompany the student summaries and reviews)
- Summaries or lists of specific information found in brochures or instructional booklets written in the target language
- Essays or reviews of literature written in the target language
- Creative writing done in the target language
- Journal entries, letters, photos, and artifacts from travel to countries speaking the target language

Mathematics

- Pieces that show a student's ability to find and solve nonroutine problems
- Examples of nonroutine problem creation to illustrate concepts
- Examples of real-life math applications (e.g., in elementary school students might create a "consumer report" on a product, conduct surveys and represent data on graphs, examine recipes, use shopping lists to compare prices, create quilts, find or create math in stories or poems, look for geometric shapes in their environment, or set up checking accounts with a class "bank")
- Student descriptions of mathematical procedures or how to solve math problems
- Written explanations of concepts with examples
- Investigations of patterns or relationships
- Application of technical documentation
- Student-created models of math concepts (such as homemade manipulatives) or specific problem types
- Student-made quizzes, sample problems, assessments
- Samples of homework, class work (puzzles, games, number books, calculator math), tests (timed tests, pretests, and posttests), projects, and research (Samples could be chosen from the beginning, middle, and end of a marking period to show progress. A student should write a reflection to cover the several samples and discuss what has been learned, how the work has improved, what was done to learn and improve.)
- Long-term projects and research into math-related topics or professions
- Daily notes and journal entries about topics such as troublesome test problems (Knight, 1992)

- Discussions of math phobias and how the student overcame them (Burke, 1993, p. 40)
- Glossary of math terms with student definitions and illustrations
- Problem-solving logs (Burke, 1993, p. 40)
- Photos or videos of class work, group projects, and presentations
- Statistics, data, graphs, blueprints, and illustrations created to illustrate mathematical concepts in applications beyond "pure" mathematics (Central Park East Secondary School, 1991)

Physical Education

- Personal wellness plans, including nutrition and exercise targets and progress
- Records of physical performance, goals, and improvements
- Videotapes of skill performance activities and following discussion and evaluation (Smith, 1997, p. 49)
- Journals of self-assessments and documentation of progress toward goals in physical performance and wellness (Smith, 1997, p. 49)
- Evidence of group projects where students discuss, design, and execute plans
- Individual projects on various aspects of sports, fitness, health topics, and physical education (Smith, 1997, p. 49)
- Evidence of participation in organized or recreational sports activities—such as team rosters, newspaper coverage, awards, records, coaches' assessments, photos, journals, parents' reflections and records
- Evidence of volunteer activities related to health and physical activity—such as coaching youth teams, working at hospitals or nursing homes, taking part in community functions that improve the health or fitness of community members
- Photos of class participation in physical activity
- Written assignments and tests on content in health and physical education courses
- Results of fitness evaluations done at school, doctor's offices, or health clubs
- Projects that integrate health and physical education into other content areas
- Certification in CPR, Red Cross swimming, or water safety or as a swimming instructor
- Successful completion of ropes courses, trust-building activities, or team problem-solving programs documented with photos and individual and group reflection

- Projects that use technology in health and physical education—for example, multimedia presentations on favorite sports or activities; using heart rate monitors, anatomy, and physiology computer software equipment to measure things such as body function and body-fat composition (Willis, 1990)

- Student-created games, dances, and physical routines

- Participation in training in conflict resolution and fundamentals of self-defense (Donahue, Marmo, & Soto, 1994, p. 3)

- Newspaper and magazine articles concerning health and fitness issues accompanied by student summaries and reactions

Science

- Depictions of significant causes and effects (In elementary classes, these could be such things as recipes, timelines, observations, and drawings from field trips; collages made from nature; and surveys.)

- Replications or validations of investigations

- Design, executions, and results of investigations that show the use of scientific methodology (For elementary students, these could be based on the KWL model.)

- Real-life applications of science, careers involving science, and misconceptions avoided through scientific understanding

- Application of technical documentation

- Journal or learning logs of daily observations and questions and resulting personal theories

- Research, results, and response to some observational questions

- Lab reports, homework, tests, projects, research

- Photos, videos, or other visual representations of work in science class

- Awards or recognition for participation in science fair or similar competitions in science and photos of displays

- Entry that shows a depth of understanding of a scientific concept through music, art, poetry, video, or other media in an original or unique way (California Department of Education, 1996)

- Printouts of e-mail and faxes received from scientific contacts in the process of scientific investigations

- Copies of Internet materials accessed in the process of research, accompanied by student summaries and reflections

- Tape recordings of interviews with professional scientists or professionals who use science in their work

- Written responses to guest speakers or field trips

Social Studies, History, and Geography

- Examples or depictions of significant causes and effects
- Explanations of current events in light of historical background
- Evidence of reading in the field, such as reading beyond the text in newspapers, periodicals, books, reference material, and original documents (This evidence could be supplied by annotated bibliographies, summaries, essays, abstracts, or response notes.)
- Real-life application of course information and investigation of possible careers using course content
- Misconceptions avoided through knowledge of history, geography, and social studies
- Journal entries of personal reactions, observations, and questions
- Reviews of news shows, dramas on TV, movies, plays, and speeches that connect to course content
- Samples of homework, class work, notes, group assignments, reports, projects, tests, class presentations, and research accompanied by student reflection and photos, videos, or illustrations when appropriate
- Photos and diaries of school or personal trips to course-related sites, museums, reenactments, exhibits, or dramas
- Creative pieces—written, visual, musical, dramatic—incorporating course concepts or events (These could include maps, brochures, games, student articles, poems, stories, graphic organizers, drawings, collages, murals, songs, crafts, skits, dioramas.)
- Artifacts showing the student's personal history, such as student-created family albums, family trees, genealogies, "All About Me" books, ethnic recipes, and family myths and traditions
- Oral histories
- Timelines
- Video or cassette recordings of interviews with local historians or people who lived through a particular era being studied
- Evidence of participation in local historical activities such as restorations, reenactments, museum exhibits, preservation efforts, and education or information programs for students or adults
- Evidence of participation in school improvement efforts, local government, school or community elections, or civic activities

Vocational and Career Preparation and Transition Courses

- Résumé
- Sample letters of application

- Reference letters
- Descriptions of jobs held
- Evidence of positive work habits such as supervisors' evaluations, timecards, commendations, and promotions
- Transcript of courses completed
- Evidence of skills developed in various courses, for example, products produced in courses such as reports, business documents, computer graphics, software programs, Web pages; photos of construction projects, rebuilt automobiles, satisfied cosmetology patrons; videos or photos of work with children in day care situations
- Artifacts that show the ability to work productively in teams, such as photos of work process and products, narratives of the process a group used and the part an individual student played, evaluations from teachers or supervisors and teammates
- Certificates of participation in career-related organizations and competitions
- Awards received in career-related competitions
- Evidence of understanding and ability to use Deming's cycle for quality—plan, do, study, act (Guidance Centre, 1994)
- Self-appraisal of career goals and aptitude for particular careers (Lincoln County School of Technology, 1996)

Ideas for Additional Portfolio Entries

- A sample of work that reflects a problem that was difficult for the student
- A sample of work that shows where the student started to figure out the problem
- A sample that shows how the student solved the problem
- A sample that shows the student learned something new
- A sample of work in which the student needs to keep searching for ideas
- Items of which the student is proud
- A sample of a comical disaster (Hamm & Adams, 1992)
- Extracurricular activities that enhance the overall picture of the student as learner
- Positive notes from the teacher
- Letters from parents to the student
- Work samples that demonstrate the uniqueness of the student as a learner

- Photos of students working in class or demonstrating learning (see pp. 107-108 in Resource A)

Commentaries

Whatever original pieces go into the collection, they should be accompanied by student commentaries that explain the original assignment and discuss the student's process for doing the work, the student's assessment of the quality of the work, and what the work demonstrates about the student's learning and progress at that point. These commentaries are invaluable for several reasons. First, they aid a reader in understanding the portfolio pieces. Second, they force the student to think and talk about the pieces he or she chose for the portfolio. Finally, such reflection on learning experiences is necessary for students to cement the learning in their minds for easy access and use later. As Mary Hamm and Dennis Adams (1992) observe, "Since students need to be involved actively in evaluating and providing examples of their own learning, they must document the probing questions they are asking, identify what they are thinking, and reflect on their understanding" (p. 105).

Students will need some guidance when they first start writing commentaries. A teacher can give them a few pertinent questions, for example:

- What was the original assignment for this piece?
- Why did you choose this sample for your portfolio?
- What do you want a reader to notice about this work?
- What does it show about your learning or progress?

A teacher might also give the students commentary forms to fill out and attach to artifacts going into the portfolio (see pp. 121-131 in Resource A). Sometimes a commentary is not needed for every piece. If several artifacts have been chosen to show the student's progress through a particular concept or type of work, one commentary for the collection of work might be enough. If students are putting samples in from all the content areas they study, perhaps one commentary per subject will suffice. If students add self-selected pieces to their portfolio collection, however, they need to be sure to have a commentary for each choice so that whoever looks at the portfolio can see the significance of the artifact. One of the most interesting things about commentaries is that as students get comfortable writing them, the commentaries become richer evidence of learning than the artifacts themselves. It is in the commentaries that we feel we are hearing the voice of the student discussing the significant learning that has taken place.

Box 2.1. Sample High School Commentary
on a Creative Experiment

Creative experiments are writing assignments in which we get to use our imaginations to respond to a topic in a unique way based on our knowledge of the material it covers. This particular creative experiment was an essay question on our unit test on Bronte's *Wuthering Heights*. We were to become the character of Catherine Linton Heathcliff Earnshaw and write an entry in her diary shortly after her marriage to Linton Heathcliff. I chose to write on this topic because I had never done a creative experiment before, and it sounded interesting. I had fun writing this entry, and it helped me to realize that all writing is not boring. At the point in time in which I did this piece, I still had problems expressing myself in essays, although otherwise my writing was pretty good. The style of this experiment helped me to show my knowledge of *Wuthering Heights* without having to worry about manuscript errors, and I found it easier to express my thoughts. I chose to include it in the portfolio for a change of pace and to show that I am a versatile writer when I need to be.

Michelle Earp, 11th grade

Box 2.2. Sample Elementary Commentary on Math Artifacts

I want you to notice that I'm a good problem solver and I'm good at multiplication. I have learned about decimals and I have learned that I can be a good math student when I focus. It will help me when I go shopping. I found that when I started 3-minute multiplication it was the most difficult.

Jennifer, age 9

Table of Contents

In addition to student work samples and commentaries, several other items should be included to make the showcase portfolio look complete and professional. No matter what the grade level of students, a portfolio needs a title page and a table of contents. To personalize the title page, young students could be asked to decorate it with drawings, and older students could be asked to find and use a quote they feel is appropriate. Students can generate the table of contents once they have organized their

Box 2.3. Sample Preface From an Elementary Student Portfolio

I'm making a portfolio because I can keep track of my work. In my portfolio I want people to see my quality work. I also want people to see how I am doing in school.

Heather, 7th grade

Box 2.4. Sample High School Preface

The purpose of my portfolio is to combine, in one place, a collection of my best written work. As I add additional samples of my work, I hope to meet my goal.

The goal that I have set for myself this year is to improve the mechanics of my writing skills. Hopefully, as I make additions to my portfolio, these skills will improve.

I have been taught in sports and other things that practice makes perfect. If I continually try to improve, then I hope to produce quality work. Quality is the commitment to continuous improvement. My writing should get better as the year goes on. This portfolio will show this.

Clark Gray

material, but we have found that it is usually a good idea for the teacher to supply a table of contents for young students or those who have not created a portfolio before. Having some uniformity in how the material is organized in the portfolio will also help the teacher when it is time to assess the student work.

Writing a Preface and an Epilogue

Portfolios that are intended to show a student's progress and growth over the course of the year also need a preface and an epilogue. The preface should be written at the beginning of the year just after the portfolios have been introduced. Teachers have asked us how students could introduce the portfolio collection before they have done it, but they are not commenting on the collected work yet. They are introducing themselves, setting a personal purpose for the portfolio, sharing a vision of quality, and discussing their goals for the year.

Box 2.5. Sample Intermediate Student's Epilogue

The important things I have learned this year are some test-taking strategies. I have learned to always go back and check over my tests, to always read the questions over first, and to read the questions before you read the passage. These strategies are important because when I take a test in high school, I will do better.

My greatest accomplishment was my reading. I have really improved on my spelling and my handwriting. I chose these because when I get a job, I will need these skills.

The subjects I enjoyed most were science, math, and reading. I chose these subjects because I like to learn and sometimes they can be kind of fun.

My greatest challenges were the end of grade test, writing and passing fourth grade. I picked these for my greatest challenges because they were hard and difficult.

In fifth grade, I hope to learn about the universe in science, about the United States, and more about nature.

David Smith, June 5, 1997

Box 2.6. Sample High School Student's Epilogue

I have learned a lot about English literature and writing this year. I have learned how to not only appreciate literature, but how to look at it from different angles to understand it better. My writing has improved so dramatically that it is incredible. Until this year I never knew that I could write or love poetry to the extent I do now. My appreciation for all types of literature has increased. I also know how to read literature in a way to make it easier to understand.

I have also met all of the goals I made for myself. My organizational skills have improved, and I now have a notebook method that is very easy to use. Also, my goal of improving my writing has been achieved, and I know this because I got an A for the third 9 weeks, meaning I had all excellent work.

I am proudest of my portfolio. It is a great record of how my skills have improved, and it is a reminder that if I try hard enough, I am capable of achieving great things.

Amanda Levine, June 1994

If a teacher has students create a self-portrait, visual or written, to explain who they are and what they hope to accomplish, the teacher can return these when students write their prefaces. These documents can be the preface or raw material for creating the preface for portfolios. Because this preface gives a view of the student at the beginning of the process, it will be useful to have students create an epilogue at the end of the process to demonstrate how they have changed and improved.

The teacher should give some guidance to students as to what to include in these beginning and ending statements. Having students answer the questions "Who are you?" and "Why are you here?" at the beginning of school can be a good way to generate the preface, which should introduce the student, state goals for the year, and discuss how the portfolio might help in reaching those goals. The answers to the questions "What have you learned?" and "How have you changed or what progress have you made toward your initial goals?" may be used as the epilogue to conclude the school year. Students may find it useful to look at prefaces and epilogues in nonfiction books to see what they include before they write their own. Even the youngest students can personalize their portfolios by introducing themselves with a self-portrait or a scripted preface.

Once the portfolio is completed, the student needs to wrap up the collection process by writing an epilogue. In this final statement from the author, the student should discuss the significant learning achieved through the grade or course. He or she should also discuss progress made toward the goals that were set at the beginning of the year or marking period. Often, the difference between the student's maturity and expression of ideas in the preface and the epilogue is amazing proof of the learning that has taken place. One evidence of this learning is the fact that the epilogue tends to be much richer and more elaborate than the student's reflections at the beginning. Once this begins to happen, the student is on the way to becoming a self-directed, reflective learner (see p. 109 in Resource A).

Including a Résumé

Another item that should be included in all portfolios is a résumé. Even the youngest students can create a résumé that lists their personal facts, strengths, and experiences (see p. 110 in Resource A). The items and sophistication on the résumé can be tailored to the age of the students. A fourth-grade teacher at an elementary school in Zionville, NC, takes pictures of her students on the first day of school. As students complete their résumés, she attaches the photos to their résumés. For secondary students, the résumé should follow a professional format and can actually be used to apply for jobs or postsecondary education. Whatever format the résumé takes, it immediately personalizes the portfolio. No two people have the same résumé! Once the portfolio becomes personal, it really belongs to the student, and the ownership will help instill the desire to create a good portfolio.

Box 2.7. Sample Sixth-Grade Résumé

Name:	Annie Murray Binning
Pets:	Chloe, 3 years old, golden retriever, yellowish white. She loves to run, jump, swim, and bark.
Hobbies:	sports—soccer, skiing, swimming, running
Collections:	seashells, beads, and soccer magazines
Awards & Honors:	making "A Team" for 2 years, OM—1994 my team placed third and 1995 my team placed first
Volunteer & Jobs:	Volunteer—American Red Cross and chores around my house (boring) Jobs—Cleaning Shook Creek Guest House
Favorites:	music—alternative, food—quiche, subject—reading, author—Jan Karon, vacation spot—Paris, France or Vancouver, British Columbia, store—The Limited or American Eagle
Person I Admire Most:	I admire many people. Some of them are Mia Hamm, Carla Berube, Michelle Akers, Carin Gabarra, Brian McBride, and Kristine Lilly (All the people above are soccer players.)

Many of the decisions about what the portfolio will look like and what it will contain need to be determined by the teacher before the process begins in the classroom with students. The portfolio planning questions of "What is the purpose of the portfolio?" and "Who is the intended audience?" can assist a teacher in thinking about what type of container and contents are most appropriate. A teacher should also be aware, however, that the more students are involved in deciding what the portfolios look like and contain, the more ownership they will feel toward the document and, therefore, the more they will be motivated to do quality work.

What Is the Process for Using Portfolios in a Classroom?

Once the teacher has made some of the initial decisions, the use of the portfolio with students follows a seven-step sequence. This sequence is the same whether the portfolios are being used for one class project or for the entire year. Because the process for developing student portfolios is consistent for students in kindergarten through 12th grade, teachers can encourage, assist, and support one another across grade levels as their students work on their portfolios.

Explain Portfolios and Their Uses to Students and Parents

This should be done at the same time that the teacher informs students and parents about the student-led conferencing, whether in a meeting or through a letter. For both students and parents, seeing actual portfolios is very useful. If no student portfolios are available, teachers can create a sample one to show, share a professional portfolio, invite local professionals who have portfolios to come to class to share them, or ask older students who have showcase portfolios to come and share them with the class. If models of student portfolios are available, they can be left on display in the classroom for students and parents to view throughout the year. In addition to gaining a vision of what a portfolio is, parents and students need to know the purpose for the portfolios, who the intended audience will be, and how, if at all, this portfolio will be evaluated and counted toward credit for completing the year. All this information should be shared to begin the process.

Set Quality Standards

The most important step in setting quality standards for class portfolios is creating a culture in the classroom that promotes and insists on quality work from students at all times. W. Edwards Deming (in Aguayo, 1990) observes that "quality is only possible when the people in the system feel secure and experience joy in what they do" (p. 50). The goal of educators involved in promoting quality work must be to create schools and classrooms where students feel secure and enjoy their learning experiences. Building this environment is not always easy, especially since many of our students learn quickly that mediocrity will suffice in school and others do not feel safe in their classes or experience delight in learning. We must persevere, however, in the larger context of focusing on quality in schools if we want students to produce specific examples of quality work, such as showcase portfolios.

Focus on Quality in the Classroom

Once a conducive environment is established, students must be made aware that the world beyond school will demand that they do consistently high-quality work. Then they need to be taught processes and methods that will enable them to do such work. The theories of W. Edwards Deming (Aguayo, 1990) offer insight into ways to achieve quality, and many of them can be adapted to the classroom. Deming defines *quality* as the commitment to continuous improvement, and if a teacher can instill this commitment in students and give them a classroom organized

Box 2.8. Barriers to Quality in the Classroom

Brainstormed by Seventh Graders
Too rushed
No second chances
No time to preview or ask questions
Family commitments
Friends
Natural disasters
Illness
Lack of materials
Teacher yells, pressures, nags
Directions unclear
Homework unfair
Teacher talks too much
No help from teacher
No help from parents

From the seventh-grade class of Suzi Loya and Jim Phieffer, Port Orchard, Washington.

to encourage goal setting and progress, the quality of students' work will increase, whether it is directly for their portfolio or not.

Because the concept of *quality* carries different meanings to different people, teachers may want to start the school year with some exploratory sessions on quality. The following lesson is a good start.

1. Students begin by thinking of a quality product or performance they have seen outside of school.
2. Then they share this item and the reasons they believe it was quality with a small group of peers.
3. Once everyone has shared, the group compiles a list of the components the quality items had in common.
4. This list is shared with the class, and the whole group creates a class list of the components of quality.
5. Once this list is completed, each student writes a definition of *quality.*
6. These personal definitions can then be compared with other definitions from the dictionary and published sources.
7. The list of quality components can be displayed in the classroom throughout the year as a reminder to students that they are working in a "quality classroom," and the personal definitions can become part of the students' prefaces for their portfolios.

Just discussing quality once during the year will not be enough to focus students on doing quality work. The teacher is merely opening the conversation on quality with the initial exercise described above.

There should be an ongoing dialogue about quality in the classroom. For example, the search for quality can become part of the regular goal setting students do. The ideas that follow can help students see ways to improve the quality of their work.

1. Students are asked to brainstorm a list of reasons why they do not do quality work in school despite the fact that they can recognize quality products and performances, as evidenced by their previous discussion of quality components.
2. Once they have the list, each person in the class, including the teacher, could take one of the reasons and set a goal to improve on that item for a week.
3. At the end of the week, the class should revisit the list and goals to see how it is doing.
4. If the class has met its goals, it could use the list to set new ones.
5. If the class has not met its goals, it could use the same ones again for another week.

Such ongoing discussions on quality will be needed to teach the process for quality work. The Deming-Shewhart cycle of continual improvement (Aguayo, 1990, pp. 114-115) clearly states what this process is, and it should also be taught, modeled, and used regularly in the classroom:

- Plan what you want to do.
- Carry out the plan.
- Study the results.
- Determine what you need to improve the next time.
- Repeat the cycle.

Students who are young or novices at a particular task can come to understand quality standards by observing teacher models. The adage "You get what you ask for" is most appropriate when dealing with quality in the classroom. If the teacher wants students to produce quality work, he or she must share finished examples of student work for students to examine and model the process for producing the pieces. When dealing with any age students, teachers need to model and provide models to ensure that students understand the criteria and process for producing quality work.

Having students view professional portfolios, a teacher's portfolio, or student portfolios is the best way to begin the discussion about what quality portfolios look like. A good way to help students verbalize quality components is to put them into small groups and give them portfolios to examine. The groups should be compiling a list of the things that make the samples quality products. Students should be asked to look at the format and the content of the portfolios because both factors contribute to overall quality. From these lists, a class list of basic requirements can evolve.

Of course, the teacher will need to guide the formation of a list of criteria to be sure that the standards are sufficiently high. The teacher may wish to give a few items in the beginning of the discussion to clarify what students should be considering or add some at the end if students omit important things the teacher plans to require. No matter what the teacher adds, the importance of having the students discuss quality portfolios first is that students will understand quality criteria and will also feel that they have had a hand in determining how their portfolios will be evaluated. Such student involvement serves to increase motivation and student responsibility in the process of developing a quality portfolio.

Develop the Habit of Reflection

Because being able to write quality commentaries to accompany work samples is a key part of creating a quality portfolio, making reflection on learning a habit is a powerful tool for improving student performance and maintaining quality standards. Students do not automatically know how to comment on their work. Teachers must help them by modeling self-reflection, teaching methods, and vocabulary for students to use in discussing their own work and by giving them plenty of practice throughout the year. Making reflection and goal setting part of the learning process and encouraging students to identify what they have learned, how they have learned, how they can use their learning beyond the classroom, and what they can do to improve can significantly raise student achievement. Research has shown that teaching students, particularly low-achieving students, to set goals enhances their sense of their own ability to learn, their academic achievement, and their interest in school (Schunk, 1990).

Through daily reflective activities that model and teach the language of self-reflection, students learn to assess their learning, appraise their work objectively, and set goals for themselves as learners. Teachers at all grade levels can start their students using reflective language from the first day of school by asking students to think of something they learned today. Initially, students won't know what to say when asked this question, and the teacher will have to model how to respond. If students do try to answer, their responses will often be about the things they made or activities that they found fun and interesting rather than the concepts, processes, and strategies they learned while involved in a task. As teachers work with students on developing their reflective skills, students learn to direct their reflections more toward the concepts, processes, and strategies that enable them to be successful students (see pp. 111-112 in Resource A).

The first step in teaching students to reflect is giving them opportunities to verbalize their thinking. Asking students to record their reflections is the next step in teaching students to reflect. Even kindergarten and early first-grade students can record their self-reflections by drawing pictures accompanied by one or two dictated sentences. Older students may need a structured format to frame their reflections and their goals when they first start writing reflections (see samples of reflection pages and guide questions in Resource A). As students develop their own vocabulary for self-reflection, reflections will become more open ended and personal, and students require less guidance.

Reflective self-assessment can also occur after specific assignments. For example, after students have finished going over a test or major assignment that has been graded, they can be asked to respond to three questions:

- What did you do well on this assignment?
- What didn't you do well?
- What strategy can you use next time to do better?

Be aware that most students have no real idea about what might be a good strategy for improving their work. Most will initially tell you that their strategy is to "work real hard" and get an A. This is not a strategy but a broad statement of optimism! They will need help identifying real strategies. For example, a struggling student, after much thought and prodding, finally came up with a strategy—to find out when tests will be given. It might not be as high level a strategy as we would hope, but, if he was coming to tests unaware and without preparing, it is a good place to start!

Involving students in this kind of focused reflection leads to goal setting and is practice for the commentaries that will accompany work in the completed portfolio. Also, if this strategy is done on a regular basis, for example with each unit test, and students are held accountable for using the strategies they identify, content learning and the caliber of student work will improve. Eventually, students should be able to answer these questions before the assignment is graded and be on target evaluating the quality of their work.

As students become involved in establishing quality standards in the classroom, motivation and responsibility increase. Students view their work realistically and set goals for improvement. The development of quality showcase portfolios then becomes the next step in establishing quality standards in the classroom because it provides a systematic method of collecting and displaying evidence of student learning and improvement.

Teach Organizational Methods

Once the portfolio process is begun, students will be required to keep up with their work so that when they compile the portfolio, they will have the necessary samples. The younger and more immature the students are the more the teacher will have to assist them in developing the habits necessary to be responsible for their work over an extended period of time. As teachers know, organization may be one of the most difficult skills for a majority of students to master.

Some ideas for organizational methods:

- Have students use daily notebooks and teach an organizational method for them to keep work in the notebooks.
- Have students keep journal entries in a daily notebook.
- Have works in progress folders in the room so students or the teacher can file work once it has been completed and evaluated the first time. These folders could be in a file cabinet, in a plastic crate, in a box, or on shelves.
- Use colored hanging file folders for the works in progress folders. Select five of each color and arrange the colors so that the same colors are always together. Label each folder with a student's name. Students can quickly locate their folders by finding the color first and then their names.
- Train students to file or keep their own work organized. If this is important in the process of developing the portfolio, the teacher will need to check to see that it is being done, give class time to do it, give students grade credit for doing it (if appropriate), and help students do it in the beginning. Even the youngest students can develop the skills to file their own work for later use if the teacher gives them the strategies and practice to learn the habit.
- Have a place to keep the portfolios safe when students are not working on them. Again, shelves or plastic crates are useful. The crates are nice for teachers who do not have shelves or who are not in a single classroom all day because they can be stacked in a corner out of the way. They are also handy when the teacher needs to carry portfolios home for evaluation.

Having the student work samples and ongoing reflections available when it is time to create the portfolio is essential. Students will not understand the significance of being organized and keeping their "stuff" until the first time they must get the portfolio ready for conferences. Brandon, a second-grade student, liked nothing better than to play and talk all day with his friends. Unfortunately, when it came to schoolwork, Brandon often "lost" his work. Most of the time, the teacher found it unfinished and stuffed in his desk. As conferencing time approached, it became apparent that Brandon was going to have difficulty organizing and completing his portfolio. Time finally ran out, and Brandon had to explain to his parents why his portfolio was incomplete. As students prepared for their at-home conference after Christmas, again Brandon's portfolio was far from complete. When it came time to put the portfolios together for the spring conference, the teacher anticipated that Brandon was going to need help again getting organized, but to everyone's surprise, Brandon jumped up, arms raised above his head, and yelled, "I'm done!" The other students, realizing the significance of this accomplishment, cheered. For most students, however, it will take only that first experience of trying to assemble a portfolio to realize the importance of being responsible for their own work. Until they see it themselves, we must help them by giving them guidance and methods for organizing the evidence of their learning.

Collect All Relevant Work Samples

Once the organizational systems are in place, students will need to know what to keep for their portfolios. It is important that a wide variety of work be available when the portfolio selection process begins. A good idea is to have students keep everything in the works in progress folder that is related to the artifacts that might eventually go into the portfolio. For example, if one portfolio entry is to represent a class project, then all stages of the work need to be kept. If the portfolio is to show progress in a student's learning, such as in writing or mastering math concepts, then anything showing stages of the process needs to be saved. If the portfolio will include different content areas, work for all of them should be saved.

Students are not used to doing this type of record keeping. They've had the teacher to do it for them! Therefore, they will need to know from the beginning that they should keep all pieces of the work in question so that when the time comes to pull the portfolio together, they will have what they need. Once the teacher tells students what they should keep, the process of organizing portfolio materials is in the hands of the students. Some students will invariably lose or fail to keep some of their work, but we must begin turning responsibility over to them. If the teacher tries to keep up with all the student work, students never really take possession of their own learning or assume responsibility. Teachers must help students establish systems and habits to organize and save necessary work samples, but resist the urge to do it all for them.

Pieces which are eventually selected for the portfolio need to be accompanied by student commentaries that explain the assignment and discuss the process for completing the task, the student's assessment of the quality of the work produced, and what the student has learned. To help students remember what the work sample was so that they will not write generic commentaries at the end, the teacher should ask students to do reflection as part of the original assignment or task. Reflecting on work while the learning experience is still fresh in their minds enables students to be more objective in the assessment of their work and write better commentaries for their portfolios. Following are some ideas for getting frequent reflections on student work before it goes into the works in progress folder:

- Before students turn in an assignment, ask them to write on it three things they would like for you to notice when you evaluate the work.
- Before students turn in an assignment, ask them to tell you what they learned by doing the work and list any questions they have about it.
- When students get an assignment back, have them write on it or on an attached piece of paper what the original assignment was, what they learned by doing it, and what they would do to improve it.
- Ask students to write on a piece of work, either before or after they turn it in for evaluation, what they did well on the sample, what they did not do so well, and what they would do to improve the quality of the work.
- Before they turn work in or after it has been evaluated, ask students to record on it what part of the work was hard for them and how they solved the difficulty they were having with it.
- Ask younger students to talk about their work samples and tell whether or not they think the samples are quality and why. Their answers could be scripted and attached to the work before it goes in the works in progress folder.

If students will record in some way how they felt about the assignment at the time they did it, they will not have so much trouble writing commentaries if that particular sample is chosen to go in the portfolio. They also are developing the vocabulary and habits of thought necessary for serious and useful self-reflection.

Select Works for Inclusion

Approximately 2 weeks before the portfolios are to be completed for evaluation, students need to know what to include in their portfolios. Up to this point, students have been saving all relevant pieces of work that reflect the learning that has taken place in the classroom over the marking period. Although they know that some pieces—a preface, a title page, and a table of contents, for example—are required for the portfolio, the

---

Box 2.9. Sample Second-Grade Table of Contents
for First Marking Period

Preface
Two Pieces of Writing
Journal
Selection from Writing Folder
Social Studies
My "Marvelous Me" Magazine
Math
Geometry Work
Science
The Life Cycle of a Butterfly
Language
"Doing Words"
Reading Partner Visit Reflection
Something I Am Proud of . . .

---

rest of the portfolio contents may not have been specified yet. In our experience, we have discovered that it is very difficult to predict everything that might be in a portfolio for a marking period because the class may not get to all we had planned. Therefore, we cannot tell students from the beginning everything that will be required in the portfolio.

Some portfolio proponents say that students should select whatever they want for their portfolios. We disagree, especially if the portfolios are intended to be part of the class assessment system and are to be shared with parents and guests to demonstrate student learning.

Students will need guidance in making selections for several reasons. First, the portfolios should reflect the curriculum that is required in the school system. Work samples need to be tied to what the particular class is studying. Second, the task of gathering, selecting, and organizing required portfolio pieces often overwhelms even the most organized student. The teacher, therefore, needs to state for students what pieces or types of samples need to be chosen from the works in progress folders to include in the portfolio. Teachers can do this by giving students the table of contents for that marking period. Other teachers list the portfolio requirements on a poster, overhead transparency, or blackboard. Quality, not quantity, is a good rule of thumb when selecting work samples for the portfolios. We suggest that teachers limit the number of portfolio selections to 8 to 12 work samples to allow students time to improve the quality of each selection. The selections may come from one or several

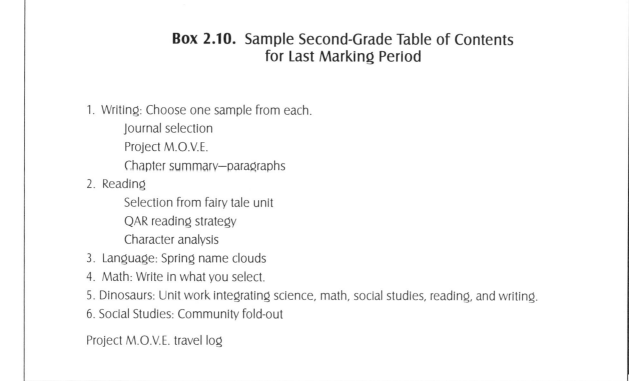

Box 2.10. Sample Second-Grade Table of Contents for Last Marking Period

1. Writing: Choose one sample from each.
   Journal selection
   Project M.O.V.E.
   Chapter summary—paragraphs
2. Reading
   Selection from fairy tale unit
   QAR reading strategy
   Character analysis
3. Language: Spring name clouds
4. Math: Write in what you select.
5. Dinosaurs: Unit work integrating science, math, social studies, reading, and writing.
6. Social Studies: Community fold-out

Project M.O.V.E. travel log

curriculum areas. If the portfolio includes too many samples, several things occur. The students become overwhelmed by the task; the teacher spends a great deal of class time helping students prepare the portfolios; and whoever looks at the portfolio becomes overwhelmed by the excessive number of portfolio entries and is tempted to rush through the collection.

Although we advocate that the teacher have a say in what is included in a showcase portfolio, we believe that students need some choices as well. If the teacher chooses all the pieces, the portfolio belongs to the teacher, not to the student. In addition, if the students are merely gathering things that the teacher wants with no freedom to add what they feel is important, they will do what students have always done—produce a "bunch of stuff" to make the teacher happy. They will not invest any of themselves in the portfolio. Student ownership is a major factor in the success of student portfolios, and the portfolio should reflect the personality of the student.

When students begin selecting work samples for their portfolios, the teacher may want to limit the students' self-selections to one or two pieces and keep the selection criteria relatively simple (See Box 2.9). Students usually select a writing sample or journal entry as their first self-selection. Gradually, as students become familiar with the portfolio selection process, the portfolio table of contents becomes less detailed and more open ended (See Box 2.10).

Another way to involve students in selecting artifacts is to demand some pieces that represent major work in the class but also ask for a representation of a type of work and allow the student to choose which specific example to include. A teacher can allow students to include optional pieces they feel are excellent work or show another side of their learning. A traditionally low-achieving high school student taught us this lesson when he asked to include an acceptance letter from a local community college, something the teacher had not even considered as a possible entry but that was absolutely appropriate. Students may wish to put in work from a class not included in the portfolio collection, awards from community and school activities, or other artifacts to demonstrate their achievements. Teachers should encourage this because it makes the portfolios the property of the students and motivates them to do the quality work necessary to produce a real showcase portfolio.

Even kindergarten students are capable of selecting items for a showcase portfolio with the teacher's help. To do this, the teacher sits on the floor with a group of four to eight children, and together they look through their works in progress folders. The students enjoy discussing and reflecting on their completed work. As the teacher selects a piece of work from a child's folder, the other children look through their folders to find a similar piece. The students and teacher then discuss what students would want to tell their parents about the selected piece. This process and discussion help students rehearse for their conferences and give the teacher an opportunity to assess students' learning. The teacher continues this activity until four or five items have been selected for the portfolios. Once students place their selections into their portfolios, the portfolios are complete and ready to share with parents.

With younger students, revising and correcting student work is minimal because most early elementary teachers assess and evaluate students' work on a daily basis. Depending on the developmental level of the student, the work may be the highest quality it can be at that time. Developing the portfolio usually involves selecting pieces, completing unfinished work, and organizing the required work into the portfolio format.

No matter the age, students need the time to go through their works in progress folders and make selections. Often there are students who realize, as a high school freshman said, "There's nothing in my works in progress folder!!!" Therefore, some class time might be needed to complete work samples or to do makeup work.

Time may also be needed for some students to revise work so that it will be acceptable for inclusion in the portfolio. This time is well used, however, because as students are going through their work for the class, they are reviewing all the content they have studied. High school students have reported that they did not need to study for exams after getting their portfolios together because they were reviewing their content throughout that process.

Assess and Evaluate Portfolios

Regardless of the method used to select material, to develop a quality portfolio, students need to be clear about the portfolio requirements and how the document will be assessed and evaluated. The best way to communicate this information is through a rubric that states the criteria and describes the quality standards for different levels of performance. Whether the portfolios are going to be used to get a grade, as they often are in middle and high school; to give assessment information about the student's learning and progress, as they often are in early elementary school; or both, a clear rubric will help students understand what they are expected to do to succeed.

If the portfolio is going to be used for assessment alone—in other words, as a tool to give a picture of a student's progress and best efforts at a given time—it can be wonderfully effective. By looking at the showcase portfolio after each marking period, the student, the parents, and the teacher can set academic goals and discuss what needs to be done to improve the student's performance. Best of all, the assessment process has been going on throughout the development of the portfolio. This aspect of portfolios is one of the strongest reasons for using them in a classroom, and a grade might not even be necessary. As Seidel and Walters (1992) state,

> Assessment is central to the process of learning, and is, therefore, inseparable from the curriculum. Portfolio assessment is not an event for the last week of the school year. The use of portfolios implies an atmosphere, a language, and a set of activities that take a major place in the life of the classroom. (p. 5)

For K-3 students, the portfolio process is more important than using the finished product for a grade. The emphasis is on collecting work samples, organizing samples, and completing necessary work at an acceptable level. Only work that has met the quality standards the class has set can be put in the portfolio. The rest of the required work will remain in the works in progress folder for the student-led conferences. Because the individual pieces have already been evaluated by the teacher, there will not be a grade on the final portfolio. Instead, the portfolio is intended to be a way to show the parents a student's level of competence and progress.

If the portfolios are going to be used to determine all or part of the students' grade for a class, the students should go through several assessment loops, using the quality criteria that the teacher and class have established. By taking the portfolio through these quality checks, students will have a greater likelihood of success at a high level. The assessments that happen before a grade is given on the portfolio are done by the student, a peer editor, and the parent or guest at the student-led conference. We do not ask that a grade be assigned in any of these three assessments, only that there be a quality check using the guide or rubric that has been established.

If the teacher uses a table of contents to help students select material for the portfolio, this can act as a check for students to use to do self-assessment and have a peer check to see if the portfolio is ready for the conference and the teacher. Older students will need a portfolio guide sheet to assist them in developing their portfolios. One type of portfolio guide spells out the minimum requirements for the portfolio to be acceptable (see pp. 113-114 in Resource A). Most teachers consider these minimum requirements to equal a B or a C. It is important that the students and the teacher discuss what an A portfolio would look like. That level of performance does not necessarily need to be described on the guide sheet, but all components on the guide sheet must be in the portfolio for it to be acceptable. So, if a student completes the portfolio and meets the descriptions on the guideline sheet, he or she has met the minimum requirements and the grade equivalent is easy to assign.

The guide sheet requires students to self-assess and peer assess the portfolio before the teacher receives it for evaluation. Both students must sign the guide sheet to indicate that the portfolio is ready for final evaluation. Only then should the teacher accept the portfolio. Regardless of the grade level, any portfolio that has something missing or is not up to quality standards is considered incomplete and returned to the student for corrections to receive a passing grade. The guide sheet method places the responsibility of the quality of the portfolio on the student and helps eliminate some of the "paper passing back and forth" that often occurs between teacher and student.

Another assessment loop that portfolios go through is the student-led conference. Having an adult see the portfolio before it is graded by the teacher is a quality check. As one middle school student lamented, "My mother can always find a spelling error!" The reason he was upset was that now the error was found, he would have to do something about it before he could turn in the portfolio for evaluation. We have found that having the conferences before the portfolios are graded is a definite plus. This prevents parents from focusing on the grade alone and allows them to help their children improve the quality of their work. It also helps teachers get the message to some parents that their child is not doing the required work in school. Because this news comes before the final grades for a marking period are given, parents have the opportunity to encourage the student to get unfinished work completed or made up. This assessment by the adult participant in the student-led conferencing improves the success rate of students and the quality of the finished portfolios. In fact, we have discovered that many students are so moti-

---

Box 2.11. Sample Holistic Rubric for Portfolio Evaluation

Not Yet Acceptable
There are not samples of evidence from each required category. Each document does not have a caption and commentary to address it. Documents do not present an argument that the required content and competencies have been learned. The portfolio does not have a professional look.

Acceptable
There is at least one sample of evidence from each required category. Most documents have captions, and all have commentaries, although some commentaries are not as thorough as necessary. The collection presents an adequate argument that the student has learned the required content and competencies. The portfolio has a professional look with only a few minor errors in format.

Excellent
There is one or more samples of evidence from each required category and artifacts in additional categories that are appropriate but not required. All entries have captions and commentaries addressing them. The argument presented by the portfolio collection is compelling in demonstrating the student's mastery of all required content and competencies. The accumulated collection and commentaries contain unanticipated insights and statements of personal learning. The portfolio meets professional quality standards.

---

vated to get the portfolios completed before their parents see them that there is little left to do to get them ready for us to grade them.

Portfolios can be documents used in the conferences but not graded or considered as part of the course grade. This happens more often in early elementary years. Older students want the portfolios to be part of how they are evaluated, however, because they work so hard on preparing portfolios that show the best work they do through the year. How much significance the portfolio grade has in the final grade for a marking period must be up to the teacher to decide. One caution, however: Do not become so focused on grading that you ruin the potential for the portfolio to be a true learning process and product.

Elements That Need to Be Considered in Evaluating the Portfolio

- Is the portfolio complete?
- Has it met the quality standards for format that the teacher and class established?

- Does it show evidence of serious thought—both critical and creative?
- Does it demonstrate the student's level of achievement of course objectives, content knowledge, and required competencies?
- Does it show evidence of sincere student reflection on learning and assessment of progress toward student goals?
- Does it show student improvement and growth?

All these elements should be clearly stated in the rubric so that the students know what the expected levels of achievement are. Collins and Dana (1993) say, "Rating portfolios is a process of making inferences and assigning value to the collected evidence. This process requires a holistic examination of the accumulated evidence and calls on the professional judgment of the person rating the portfolio" (p. 18). Without a rubric, this process can become very difficult. The format of the rubric, however, is up to the teacher and class using it. The rubric might be holistic, giving a description of the levels of performance (see Box 2.11), or analytical, breaking the portfolio down into its parts for evaluation.

Additional Tips for Teachers as They Assess or Evaluate Portfolios

- If you are teaching more than one class that will be doing portfolios, stagger turn-in times. For example, have the portfolios from one class due on Monday, another class on Wednesday, and so on. This will save you from being overwhelmed by an enormous stack of portfolios all at once.

- Give students class time to do peer assessment. Give them instructions on what to look for and discuss the importance of the quality assurance person in the production of quality products in the world beyond school. Have peer assessment at least a day before the portfolios are due so that students can correct errors peer assessors find without suffering a late penalty on their portfolios.

- If you are using a guide sheet with the signatures of the author and peer assessor, do not even look at a portfolio that has not been self- and peer assessed or does not have the signatures of both students. If you look at one where the self- and peer assessments are not complete, the quality is usually not up to standards and you will have to look at it again anyway. Return it immediately to the student to complete the assessment and sign the guide sheet.

- Create an evaluation sheet of the things that should be in the portfolio. Have a sheet for each student portfolio and check items off as you read them in the portfolio. This will help you be consistent with each portfolio. One fascinating thing about student portfolios is that they are unique to the child, interesting to read, and sometimes so enthralling that a teacher forgets to look for each required element. Once the evaluation sheet is complete, it can be placed in the front of the portfolio to report your evaluation and comments to the student.

• Decide what errors you will insist that students correct before the portfolio can be acceptable. Write these down before you begin to evaluate portfolios so that you will remember them and be consistent with all students.

• Use removable sticky notes to make comments on student work. If the individual pieces are finished products, teachers should not write on them, but students do need to know what the teacher thought. Remark on errors and especially on good work samples; sticky notes are a good way to do that without defacing the student work.

• Use a pencil to mark lightly typos or errors in format that a student might be able to correct without rewriting or retyping the entire piece. Doing so shows your respect for the student's work and effort while indicating that errors need to be corrected.

• Write with a colored pen directly on pieces that are not acceptable so that students will have to do them again, and you will know that revisions or corrections have taken place.

• If you really want quality work from all students and the portfolios are an important part of a student's grade, hand back unacceptable portfolios and insist that they be fixed. This may seem a very time-consuming task at the beginning of the year, but once students know that you will insist that they do good, complete work, they will try harder to meet that standard the first time, and the returned portfolios will be few and far between. If you plan to do this, be sure that you have enough time to return a portfolio and have the student get it back in before a final grade must go in. It is also a good idea to look first at the portfolios of students you think might be having trouble with the work so that you can return them immediately if necessary.

Teacher evaluation of portfolios is time-consuming and will be difficult at first because it is a new process. The rewards, however, are great. First of all, you will enjoy reading the student work and especially enjoy the commentaries because they will enable you to get to know the students as you never have before. Sometimes the commentaries become longer than the actual work and ultimately more valuable than some of the content in encouraging long-term learning for students who really are engaging in assessing their own efforts and results. Reading through a student's portfolio is a conversation with the person behind the work, and as you respond, you are participating in authentic assessment, mentoring, and coaching with that young learner.

Equally important, if you insist on quality portfolios and make it possible for students to learn and practice the skills necessary to achieve quality work, you will get better work and more learning of content by more students than with traditional methods of evaluation. Hamm and Adams (1992) concur: "Portfolios provide a powerful way to link learning with assessment. They can provide evidence of performance that goes far beyond factual knowledge and offers a clear and understandable picture of student achievement" (p. 105).

From the first discussions of what a portfolio is, should look like, and should contain, the students and teacher are in a dialogue about student learning and achievement. As the students discuss the quality criteria for a professional portfolio, learn to organize and save their own work, select pieces for the portfolio with the teacher's guidance, and write commentaries about their work and learning, the dialogue continues. When they self-assess their final portfolios with the rubric, and then have a peer read and comment on their portfolios, they are taking an active role in looking at their own progress. As Seidel and Walters (1992) assert,

> Students are central to the process of portfolio assessment. What makes a portfolio a document richer than a simple collection of final products is the contribution students make as they share their thoughts about the work they've done. In this way, the process of reflection and student self-assessment of work is, in itself, an opportunity for learning as well as an invitation to students to become aware and in control of their education. (p. 5)

Planning and Preparing Student-Led Conferences 3

Although most student-led conferences are not scheduled until near the end of the grading period or term, it is essential that the teacher think through the student-led conferencing process well in advance of the actual conference date to ensure a successful conference experience for students, parents, and teachers.

The ideas offered here are suggestions based on the experiences of teachers at all grade levels. Teachers will want to modify ideas to suit their unique assignments and the developmental level of their students. Samples of some generic and more specific handouts used in actual classrooms are included in Resource A in hopes that they will assist teachers in creating forms appropriate to their own classes. The material that follows is organized according to the sequence of preparing for conferences and questions that teachers have asked as they helped students get ready to meet with parents and guests.

In Elementary Schools

When and Where Will We Conduct the Conferences?

We recommended setting aside three dates during the school year for student-led conferences. In most elementary schools, the first conference date is already set in the school calendar and occurs sometime in October. If the school year is divided into four 9-week grading periods, teachers can plan for students to share their portfolios with their parents two more times, once in a home conference at the end of the second marking period in December, and once more at a second school conference in the spring or at the end of the third marking period. In school systems that operate on 6-week rather than 9-week marking periods, teachers recognize that the effectiveness of the student-led conference diminishes if they expect parents to come every 6 weeks; therefore, we recommend that schools schedule no more than two conferences at school during the year. It is important not to overwhelm parents with too much of a good thing!

Some Possibilities for
Scheduling Conferences

- Schedule the first student-led conference with younger students (grades K-3) in 20-minute intervals and with no more than one to two conferences going on at the same time in the classroom. For the second school conference, more than two conferences can be happening at one time.
- Older students may need 30 to 40 minutes to conference. As one fourth-grade teacher stated, "Thirty minutes seems to be just the right amount of time to cover what the child wants but not overwhelm the parents."
- Schedule conferences on predetermined conference days from 11:00 a.m. to 7:00 p.m.
- Schedule conferences one or two evenings from 5:00 p.m. to 8:00 p.m.
- Schedule conferences on teacher workdays or "banked time."
- Be flexible with conference times and provide a makeup conference date. Sometimes parents are unable to attend the scheduled conference and need to reschedule. Use the time before and after school to reschedule.

The most logical place to hold conferences at the elementary level is in the classroom or a student's designated homeroom. The elementary classroom provides a perfect backdrop for the student-led conference. Preparing the classroom is an important aspect of the conference in the elementary school and should begin on the first day of school. The classroom should be child centered, attractive, and inviting. It should reflect the individual personalities of the students; the learning that has taken place over the marking period; and an emphasis on quality work and quality standards. Parents need to be alerted to the fact that they are entering the child's world. Teachers can make this point by putting a welcome sign on the door stating something like "We are a community of learners. As you walk through our door, remember to view our world through the eyes of a child."

Student work too big to be placed in portfolios can be displayed on walls and bookshelves around the room. Videotapes of students working or giving presentations can be set up to run during the conferences. Student learning centers can be set up for students to demonstrate activities. Once the conferences are over, displays and collections of student work can be dismantled, and the process of preparing the room for the next student-led conference begins again.

Some Possibilities for
Preparing the Classroom

- Use the classroom walls and bookshelves to create a gallery of student work.
- Set up displays, videos, or sample workstations for students to discuss or demonstrate what they have been doing in class.
- Play soft music to encourage quiet discussions between parents and children.
- Encourage a "celebration" atmosphere by providing juice and cookies to all conference participants.

In Middle Schools and High Schools

The when and where of conducting student-led conferences can be two of the more daunting questions about the process in secondary schools because of the number of students a teacher might see in a day. The reality of organizing conferences for 100 students makes early planning of the logistics imperative.

Deciding when to schedule conferences can be complex. First, like the elementary teacher, the high school teacher must decide how many conferences to try to conduct in a year and when they might occur in relation to report cards coming out. High school teachers have found that two conferences a year are all their students can manage, although parents often ask for more! The best time in relation to report cards has proven to be right before the end of the first and third marking periods in a two-semester, four 9-week school year. For schools on 6-week schedules or block scheduling, one conference around the end of October and one in March or April works well. Having the conference before report cards come out is important because it allows parents to see what their children are or are not doing in relation to course requirements and encourages those who are behind to catch up before the grades are final.

The other part of the when question has to do with when in the school day to schedule these conferences. Unlike elementary schools, middle and high schools do not usually have conference days set aside. The only times the teacher might talk to parents are a few minutes during an open house at the beginning of the year and when the student is doing poorly enough academically or has discipline problems severe enough to warrant a major parent-teacher conference. In secondary school, the idea of a regular conference to discuss what the students are doing right is new and will have to be introduced into time schedules.

Some Possibilities for
Scheduling Conferences

- Have conferences during the regular class periods when you have the students.
- Have conferences one or two evenings from 5:00 p.m. to 8:00 p.m.
- Use a teacher workday or "banked time" for conferences.
- Have makeup conferences before or after school for parents who cannot come at the official time.

Where to conduct conferences also becomes an issue when one realizes that a classroom meant to hold 1 teacher and 30 students will not accommodate 60 parents at the same time. The teacher will need to arrange a larger area for the conferences, and these types of spaces are often busy and scheduled far in advance. Therefore, planning early in the year will be necessary to ensure having a space for the conferences that is comfortable and suitable.

Some Possibilities for
Location of Conferences

- Arrange to use the school library, if possible. It is an environment that encourages orderly, intellectual conversations about learning.
- Arrange to use the cafeteria. The environment is not quite as formal as the library, but there are tables, which are essential for the students to display their portfolios well.
- Any large classroom or common room that offers places to sit and tables or large desks will work.
- If you schedule appointed times in the evening, you might be able to use your own classroom, depending on how many conferences are going on at once. For the rescheduled conferences before or after school, you should be able to use a regular classroom.

Whether you are an elementary teacher scheduling 30 conferences or a high school teacher arranging 100 conferences, meeting the schedules of parents is not easy. Therefore, whatever schedule you use for conferencing, parent understanding of the significance of the process and parental cooperation is crucial.

How Should We Invite and Involve Parents?

Even though parents receive the dates and times of the conference at the beginning of the year at the parents' information meeting (see Chapter 1), they need a formal invitation as the conference time draws near. Sending an invitation also gives students an opportunity to communicate the importance of the event to their parents.

Personal Invitations

Having students write personal invitations to their parents is class time well spent. Parents naturally respond positively to a special hand-written invitation from their child. For example, one fifth grader wrote to her mother,

> Dear Mommy,
>   I am so excited about my portfolio conference that I will be giving you on Thursday, March 19th from 6:30 to 8:30 p.m. It will be held in Mrs. Alls' room. I am looking forward to showing off my best work to you. Just in case you try to get out of coming, let me tell you now you're coming if I have to drive you because I have worked too hard. I know you won't be at work because you get off at 5:30 so don't forget. It is going to be so much fun having you here to see my work. Please fill out the RSVP card at the bottom and return by Monday.
>   Love,
>   Lashonda

Lashonda's mother wrote back saying, "I'll be there. I wouldn't miss it for the world." Younger students can write very powerful invitations that communicate their desire to have their parents attend, even if the spelling is still at the inventive stage. The following invitation to the first fall conference is from Susan, a second grader.

> Dear mom and dad Plese come at 7:00–7:30.
>   Plese come to my confins. You will see my poutfoleoe.
>   I am going to showe you around the room. Love, Susan

If letter writing is part of the curriculum, the students' invitations can serve the purpose of teaching a content skill as well as informing parents of conferences. Teachers have found that having the students extend the invitation is the key to getting parents to school. They may not come for the teacher, but they will come for their children!

If class time does not allow for writing a personal invitation, a form letter may be used. In either case, the student should personalize the invitation by adding the appropriate information—who is to be invited, when and where the conference will be held, a personal note restating the purpose and significance of the conference, and the student's signature. This invitation letter should also include a response section to be returned to the teacher (see pp. 115-118 in Resource A). The response portion allows the teacher to know whether the parents are or are not coming at the designated time, and permits the parents to ask for an alternative appointment if they cannot come. Elementary teachers often attach a letter to the child's invitation reminding parents of the purposes and benefits of having the conferences with their children and giving them some tips for helping the children discuss their learning. The teacher will need to get the invitation material out at least 2 weeks before the conferences are scheduled and be persistent about having an answer from all parents, even if it means calling parents on the phone.

When Parents Can't Come

Despite the fact that student-led conferencing will get more parents to school than you ever hoped, the reality is that all will not be there. For many reasons, often beyond the control of the student, 100% parent participation is sometimes impossible. Knowing that, we must be humane and build in ways to have meaningful conferences for students whose parents are not there. At one elementary school, the teachers discussed this problem at great length. In one classroom, the only family member who was able to come for Ricky, a third-grade student, was his 16-year-old brother. Teachers decided that it was best for Ricky to have a student conference with someone who knew and cared about him, and agreed that Ricky's brother could come. On the night of the conferences, Ricky sat proudly at his desk and shared his portfolio with his brother, who was very interested and supportive of Ricky's learning.

Flexibility is also important in scheduling conferences with middle and high school students. In some instances, older students may not be living at home or may have other extenuating circumstances that prevent parents from coming. Therefore, teachers need to allow the student to invite an adult other than a parent to take part in the conference. This person should be someone who cares about the student and is over 21 years of age. We have seen successful conferences between secondary students and grandparents, older siblings, aunts and uncles, and, in one case, a live-in boyfriend. For high school students, conferences with adults other than their parents are sometimes even better preparation for their future experiences with job, college, and scholarship interviews.

Regardless of the grade level of the student, the teacher can make this type of conferencing setup easier for the student by letting all the adults in the school and school system know that students may be inviting them to stand in for parents. Our system administrators, building administrators, media specialists, guidance counselors, fellow teachers, custodians, and cafeteria staff have always been delighted and honored to be invited to a student's conference. We have even had school board members and parents of students who were involved with conferences from years past volunteer to be surrogate parents for students who needed them.

No matter who sits with the students for the conference, and of course parents are preferred, each student must have a conference with a significant adult who cares about him or her. One way to ensure this is to require the conference as a prerequisite for receiving a grade or credit for completing the class. A teacher may need to be stubborn but sensitive about seeing that each student has a conference, but the diligence pays off. This was brought home to one high school teacher who had first insisted that the students have conferences with their parents. When Nathan, a quiet young man in a basic senior class, announced that he had no one to conference with, the teacher immediately assumed he was trying to get out of doing a conference at all. When questioned, Nathan explained simply that his dad had been in an auto wreck and broken his back and his mother was staying with him at a hospital 100 miles away while Nathan took care of his younger brothers. The teacher, feeling guilty for jumping to conclusions, helped Nathan arrange a conference with a favorite teacher. The conference went well, and Nathan was very pleased to receive a letter from his invited guest telling him how impressive his conference had been. All students deserve the opportunity to have a conference and will benefit from doing so.

Parent Tips for Conferences

Another way to involve parents and guests positively in the conferences is to provide them with some tips on how to help students conduct a quality conference. Especially at the elementary level, parents appreciate some lead questions to use when their children get stuck. A few simple questions can be very useful:

- Tell me about this piece or assignment.
- What did you have to do for this assignment?
- What skills did you have to use to complete the assignment?
- What do you think you did well?
- If you had to do this assignment again, what would you do to improve it?
- What did you learn by doing this?

These tips can be included on letters home to parents that might accompany invitations to the conferences or on an information handout for parents to get when they arrive for conferences (see Box 3.1, and p. 119 in Resource A).

Box 3.1. Sample Parent Handout for Intermediate Grades

Welcome to our first student-led conference of the school year! The students have worked very hard to prepare for this day. Your child will be sharing his or her portfolio. The work samples in the portfolio represent all areas of the curriculum and incorporate many skills. As your child shares his or her portfolio, you might want to ask the following questions:

Tell me about this piece or assignment.
What did you have to do?
What skills did you have to use?
What would you do next time to improve this piece?

You may notice that some of your child's work is not in the portfolio. Although we have worked for several weeks, some students have difficulty organizing and completing work on time. Sometimes the work is not in the portfolio because the quality of the work is poor. These portfolios are showcase portfolios and only A and B work is present. If you are interested in seeing additional student work, ask your child to show his or her works in progress folder. Please remember that this is a learning experience, and your child will improve each 9 weeks.

Following the conference, I am asking all parents to write a letter to their child commenting on the student-led conference. Please address the letter to your child in care of Ms. Barnett and send or mail the letter back to school. The children love hearing your reaction to the conference! Thank you for your support!

Parent Information Handouts

Giving parents an information handout as shown in Boxes 3.1 and 3.2 at the conferences will involve them in the process by helping them understand what they are to do and what they should expect to see in the student portfolio. For intermediate, middle, and high school students, a list of what the portfolio and works in progress folders should contain is very useful in holding students accountable and alerting parents when student work is incomplete. Such a list can also guide parents in helping students complete course requirements. We have found that this list often eliminates the need for additional conferences with parents about what a student might need to do to pass a class or catch up when having missed work.

Parents and Guests Helping to
Document Conferences for Students

Parents and guests will also be involved in helping to document the conference for the student. They need to understand that because the teacher will not be sitting with them during the conference, he or she will be depending on a written reflection from the adult in the conference to record the child's successful completion of the task. Therefore, in this method of reporting student progress to parents, the parents are much more involved than when they receive a report card. In fact, their collaboration in student-led conferencing is essential.

Part of the teacher's preparation for the conferences is to create a format for parents or guests to use to give students and teachers feedback on conferences. There are numerous ways to do this. Parents can be asked to write a letter to the student (see p. 120 in Resource A). We have found this to be an excellent way for students to receive support and information from their conferences. Some schools ask parents to respond immediately on the back of their handout and leave the page with the teachers. If parents want to have more time to respond, they can send the reflection back within the week. Some parents may be reluctant to write a letter, and in some cases may be functionally illiterate. We have found, however, that if parents understand that the documentation is for the child, they will go to extreme lengths to do it. One father, who was illiterate, dictated his response to another child in the family and signed it with his X! At Fisher Park School in Ottawa, parents and guests were asked to write final reflections on conferences in "The Giant Book," a huge sign-out book that seventh- and eighth-grade students had created.

Whatever method the teacher plans to use to get documentation from the adults who take part in the conferences, it is helpful to give some prompts and sentence starters for parents and guests to use to respond to students. Some of the following starters work well:

- I was really proud of you when . . .
- You do _____ really well.
- Keep up the good work on . . .
- I know that sometimes you have difficulty with . . . , but . . ."
- I am glad to see that you are taking an active role in your education but . . .
- Some ways I can help you are . . .
- I really enjoyed your conference because . . .
- One thing I believe you can improve for next time is . . .

Box 3.2. Sample Parent Handout From a
High School English Class

What to Look for at Our First Conference

Dear Parents and Guests,

Welcome to the first student-led conference of the 1997-98 school year, and thank you for joining us today. As you look at your student's work, please keep in mind that the student and the community of learners to which (s)he belongs are both "works in progress." We have spent most of the first 8 weeks together getting to know each other and setting up the ways we will work for the rest of the year. The portfolios of best work are just begun, but we are delighted to share our work with you and hope you enjoy seeing what we are doing.

Following is a list of the kinds of documents you will see today and what the students should have in each folder. If your student is missing certain items, ask about them. Some have not turned in all the required work and need some encouragement or motivation to be more conscientious in the future. If all items required for the portfolio are not in it yet, the student has until the end of this week to complete the work. Your student should show you:

A daily notebook that includes

- A student work record showing pop quiz scores (daily checks on reading and comprehension of class discussions—10 is a perfect score, and we have had seven quizzes this marking period), notebook evaluations (two so far this year), daily work and homework turn-in dates, absences, and tardies
- Daily entries of class activities
- Notes
- Daily work
- Handouts, dated and in order

A works in progress folder that includes
- A name card
- A diagnostic essay with correction sheet
- One reading card with corrections
- One process expository paragraph with corrections
- One unit test

A portfolio that includes
- A preface
- A résumé
- One reading card with corrections
- One sample of creative or reflective writing with a commentary
- One unit test with commentary

When fourth and fifth graders who had done student conferences were asked what advice they would give to students who are getting ready to do theirs, they said the recipe for success was

> 1 cup of seriousness
> ½ cup of good work
> 3¼ cups of non-nervousness (Roberts, 1996)

They are right on target. If students have been properly informed from the beginning of the school year, have collected work samples, have focused on improving the quality of their work all along, and have been doing reflections, they should be serious and have some good work for their portfolios. The only thing left is to help them prepare so that they will not be nervous.

Getting portfolios ready is the major part of preparing for the conference and will demand some class time (see Chapter 2), but other things must be done as well. If the class is self-contained, 2 weeks should be sufficient time to prepare for the student-led conference. If, however, the class meets only one period a day, the teacher may need to allow 3 weeks of lead time to help students prepare for the conferences. The following timeline may be helpful to teachers in planning for upcoming student-led conferences.

Two to three weeks before the conferences:

- Develop the list of work samples required for the student portfolio. Be sure to include one or two areas for student-selected work.

- Create the rubric to evaluate the portfolios.

- Give each student a copy of the portfolio guidelines and rubric and discuss what students need to do to complete their portfolios and prepare for the conferences.

- Have each student write a preface. Young students may include a self-portrait with two or three dictated sentences for a preface.

- Have students reflect and write about their role as learners and how they have met or progressed toward their learning goals.

- Model the process of selecting work samples from the portfolio guidelines and organizing the work in the portfolio.

- For self-contained classrooms, set aside 20 to 30 minutes a day to work on the portfolio. Classes meeting one period a day or every other day will need at least one full class period to work on preparations. Remember, students need time to select, rework, revise, and do pieces to meet established quality criteria.

- Have students write a letter to their parents or guests inviting them to the conference. Invitations from elementary students should have a note from the teacher explaining the purpose of the student-led conference, and all invitations need a response portion for parents or guests to sign confirming their attendance.

One week before the conferences:

- Call parents who have not responded to the conference notes.
- Put the finishing touches on the portfolios and write commentaries or reflections for entries (see pp. 121-130 in Resource A).
- Create a "Portfolio Visit Sheet" for people who look at a student's portfolio to sign, date, and comment on the portfolio (see p. 131 in Resource A).
- Meet with students individually or in small groups to review portfolios.
- Have students write their scripts for their conferences (see pp. 132-133 in Resource A).
- Have students practice protocol for welcoming and introducing parents and guests to the teacher.
- Model and practice conducting a conference using portfolios.
- Prepare parent handouts, a sign-in sheet (see p. 134 in Resource A), a sign-up sheet for additional conferences, and reflection sheets or a "Giant Book" for parents to sign out and comment on conferences.
- If you like, send a final reminder to parents that includes some ways they can help their children conference successfully.

The day before the conferences:

- Clean up the classroom or be sure the conference site is ready.
- If you are using a classroom, arrange desks into conference tables (four desks together) to allow students room to display their portfolios properly and encourage discussion.
- Place the portfolios and works in progress folders on the students' desks or in a central location.
- Place reading books or novels and other resources on tables for students to refer to as they share their portfolios.
- Have students prepare a thank you card to give to their parents or guests (see p. 135 in Resource A).
- Address any last-minute details such as welcome signs, student displays, and refreshments.
- Be sure all students will have someone to conference with.

The day of the conferences:

- Greet parents and/or guests.
- Enjoy watching the students conduct their conferences.
- Speak to any parents of students who are struggling to see if they wish to have another conference.
- Be sure students give out their thank you cards as parents and guests leave.
- Celebrate!

Agendas, Scripts, and Practice

Students can use the table of contents developed by their teacher to organize their portfolios and prepare for their conferences. This same table of contents can serve as a format for their conferences. Having an agenda gives even the youngest student more control over the conference and, therefore, the confidence to say, as one first grader did to her mom, who was reaching immediately for the student's portfolio, "We'll get to that in a few minutes!" Middle and high school students should also develop a script to follow during their conferences. The teacher can help with this process by supplying a list of the major work from the grading period and any other topics that should be shared with parents or facilitating a class discussion to create a list of key items to be discussed.

Younger students may need practice in showing their parents around the classroom to explain learning centers or activities they use. One teacher in Michigan created a visual script map for her students and posted it on the wall of the room. In addition, there were footprints on the floor to show where the students should take their parents. A kindergarten teacher in Florida had her students prepare and practice a math lesson with manipulatives to share with their parents. This lesson was one they had done with her, and she said she heard her words and tone of voice all over the classroom on the night of conferencing as students "taught" their parents math (J. Chapman, personal communication, February 15, 1996). As you can see, there are many possibilities for students to demonstrate their learning in developmentally appropriate ways. At middle and high schools, students may wish to teach a lesson as well, do a presentation, explain a group project display, play a musical instrument, show and discuss a videotape of a presentation or class activity, or demonstrate computer skills to their parents. The portfolios are the major document for the learning artifacts, but they are not the only way to share learning and quality performances with parents. Regardless of what is part of the student-led conferences, students will need to have their agendas planned and practiced so that everything will go smoothly.

Whatever the age or maturity level of the students, few have ever been in this kind of conferencing situation and will need some modeling or examples to help them develop their scripts and anticipate what the conferences will be like. A videotape of a model conference is one way of demonstrating the process to students. Once scripts are developed, some students will need to role-play with classmates or the teacher to practice for their conferences. The maturity and self-confidence of the students should determine how much actual practice they need before they lead conferences with their parents or guests. Things such as how to introduce parents or guests to the teacher and the importance of eye contact, tone of voice, and pacing are skills few students have, regardless of age, but they are skills they will need to behave in an appropriate manner. Therefore, the preparation should involve instruction on good conferencing as well as creating a plan for the content of the conference.

Reflecting on Progress and Goals

In addition to preparing work to show, students need to do self-reflection on their work and work habits. If a system has graduation expectations for students, for example, students may reflect on how they are making progress toward those expectations. If students have been keeping up with their own work habits by tracking absences, tardies, when work was turned in, and evidence of being responsible, self-directed learners, the reflections should address their progress. Such reflection can be based on the goals students set for themselves at the beginning of the marking period and their progress toward these goals, but it should also include a comprehensive look at their learning. Reflecting before the conference in preparation for it will lead logically to reflecting after the conference in preparation for the next grading period and its new challenges and goals.

These reflections should be incorporated into the conference script as topics for discussion. As teachers at Atkins Middle School said in their debriefing of the first student-led conferences, the reflections were the most important and informative part of the process for them and the parents and guests. In the daily reflections, they saw what students were learning and what they were confused about. In the summary reflections for the portfolios, they saw what significant learning students had gained. Most important, in the reflections before the conferences, they saw the students taking more pride and responsibility for their work as well as beginning to articulate areas where they needed to improve (D. Blanton, personal communication, May 1, 1998).

*Some Possible Reflection Questions
for Elementary or Middle School*

- As a reader, how have you improved? Problem solver? Writer?
- The thing I am most proud of is . . .
- The thing that I need to continue to work on is . . .
- My impression of _____ grade is . . .
- In social studies (communications, math, science), I have learned . . . . I need to continue to work on . . . . Something I have noticed is . . .
- I have met my goals by . . . . Next time I need to work on . . .
- What have been my greatest challenges?

*Some Possible Reflection
Questions for High School*

- What was done best?
- What was the most satisfying and why?
- What were my greatest challenges?
- What progress have I made on my goals, and what strategies did I use?
- How can I show my progress?
- What plans do I have for future improvement?

Summary reflections are the best possible way for teachers and parents to "hear" students' metacognition. We often assume we understand what students are learning and thinking about their learning, but until we go to the source, we don't really know. As students prepare to talk about their portfolios and demonstrate their learning, it is essential that they reflect and self-assess to have serious and substantive conferences that will give all of us the insight we need to help them progress.

How Can I Be Sure Students Discuss the Required Curriculum?

One of the greatest concerns to those of us who use portfolios and student-led conferencing is making sure that the portfolio contents and student conferences accurately represent all areas of the curriculum we are required by our districts or states to teach. It takes only one time for a student to announce, "I don't have anything for math!" for teachers new to the portfolio process to recognize that daily lesson plans must include a variety of opportunities for students to document all areas of the content. If we want to be sure the portfolios do in fact show the curriculum, we must be certain that students have samples from all areas of the curriculum in their works in progress folders.

It is also disconcerting to hear parents say after a conference that they thought the kids were doing fun things in class, but wondered if they were learning math, science, or another subject area they did not see. To avoid this misconception that student tasks or interdisciplinary units are fun but without substance, teachers must be sure that students know why they are doing what teachers ask them to do in class. In other words, students need to know what the learning objectives are for the lessons teachers teach. They should to be able to discuss what they are learning or practicing in their daily class work and major projects. Even the youngest students should be using the vocabulary of the required curriculum to reflect on and discuss their work. If they are used to being accountable for the curriculum and they know what they are supposed to learn on a regular basis, they will be able to discuss their learning with parents and guests and make the connections to the required curriculum. When Jennifer, a first grader, can explain her science picture to her father by naming and defining the atmosphere, lithosphere, biosphere, and hydrosphere, the teacher has been successful in teaching the curriculum!

Another way to be sure that parents and guests see that the classroom activities do address the curriculum is to have signs accompanying learning centers, student work samples, and project displays that state what content objectives were addressed. For example, parents may not realize that in the study of frogs, an obvious science topic, second graders were also working on math graphing skills, language arts research skills, and an art project. If the display of the frog projects has a sign showing the content objectives in each area that was studied, parents will see the curriculum as their children show them around the classroom. The signs can also be a prompt to help the students remember to talk about what they learned by using the proper terminology. If students can talk about their learning in all content areas and the connections between the student work and curriculum are clear to parents, they will be getting a much better idea of what is required, what their children are learning, and how well they are progressing toward the expected standards.

How Do We Plan So Parents Who Have More Than One Child at the School Can Attend All the Conferences?

Whenever student-led conferences are a schoolwide event, teachers must be sensitive to the fact that some parents may have to attend the conference of more than one child. Taking this into consideration, teachers may want to arrange with their principals to work from 11:00 a.m. to 7:00 p.m. instead of the traditional school hours of 8:00 a.m. to 3:00 p.m. This flexible schedule works particularly well in most elementary schools, where the first conference is predetermined by the district or county calendar. By extending the workday, conferences can be scheduled to suit parents' needs better.

Another way of increasing parent involvement is to hold evening conferences between the hours of 6:00 and 8:00 p.m. Parents are invited to come to school anytime during those hours. The 2-hour block also allows parents to meet with more than one child. Sometimes conference times conflict and parents have to split up, each taking a child, or in the case of a set of twins in Susan Barnett's class, the mother decided to conference with each twin separately while the other child waited in the hallway. After trying schoolwide conference night for the first time, teachers at Union Hill Elementary School considered scheduling their conferences for different grade levels on different nights to accommodate the needs of parents and to involve more parents in the conferencing process.

What About Brothers and Sisters at Conferences?

A problem that often arises when working out the logistics of student-led conferences is what to do with siblings during the conference. We recommend that teachers clearly state in a letter to parents early in the school year, and then again as the conference draws near, that because this is a very special time for the child, parents will need to make arrangements for brothers and sisters to stay at home or with friends. In most cases, parents recognize the significance of the student-led conference and make some kind of child care arrangements, but that is not always possible. Another way to handle this problem in the case of schoolwide conferences is to have teacher assistants and other support staff provide temporary child care. If formal child care has not been set up at the school, a teacher may need to step in and hold a baby or entertain a toddler so that the student can conduct an effective conference.

A similar distraction for quality conferences can be the behavior of students who are waiting to have their conferences. Sometimes, students, with a little guidance, can take care of this problem themselves. At one elementary school, prior to holding their first student-led conferences, teachers were very nervous about students misbehaving when not involved in their own conferences. Such behavior had been a pattern during parent-teacher meetings and other school gatherings. To combat this problem, teachers included instructions for how students were to act while they waited for their own conferences, during the conferences, and after the conferences as part of the conference preparation. Teachers stressed that by exhibiting positive behaviors, students would show their support for other students as they conferenced with their parents. On conference night, as students began arriving for their conferences, teachers were amazed at the change in the atmosphere of the school. Throughout the building, students chatted quietly with friends and family as they waited in hallways outside classrooms as their brothers and sisters conducted their conferences with their parents. Nowhere in the building were children running up and down hallways misbehaving. The relevancy of the task and the authentic nature of the student-led conferences had positively affected student behavior.

For middle and high school teachers, the question of what other students are doing while some are conferencing comes up as well. In our experience, this has not really been a problem, even when the conferences were going on during a high school class period. Students who were not conferencing were in other parts of the library or cafeteria preparing for their own conferences or working on class assignments for upcoming units.

How Can We Coordinate so Parents Come to One Conference That Represents Work Collected From More Than One Class or Teacher?

It is improbable to think that parents and students can conduct a separate conference in every subject area. Therefore, teachers need to coordinate their efforts to contribute to one conference. For example, in schools where students have different teachers for various subjects and only a few teachers are doing portfolios and conferencing, teachers need to ask their students if they are being required to do a portfolio in another class. If some of them are, then the teacher needs to make contact with these other teachers to arrange a way to have only one portfolio container for those students. That container can hold artifacts from several classes. When conferencing time arrives, the student has one conference to discuss the work from all classes required in the portfolio.

In situations where whole teams, grade levels, or schools are using portfolios and conferencing, the coordination will be more complex and extensive. For ideas on how several middle and high schools have managed this, see Chapter 4.

How Do We Document and Reflect on the Conferences?

On the day of the conferences, teachers can document the student conferences in several ways. One way is by setting up a videocamera in a corner of the classroom and letting it run throughout the conference time. Other teachers may feel more comfortable using a still camera and taking snapshots of students sharing their portfolios with their parents. If the teacher takes photos, duplicates of these could be put in the student portfolio with reflections on the conference. Having parents sign in and out of the conferences will document who took part and can help check to see that all students have had a conference.

The most important way to document student conferences is through reflections by the student, the parent or guest, and the teacher. It is important to document that a conference took place and to supply feedback for students so that they will know how they did and can improve for future conferences. As long as these objectives are met, it does not matter how the documentation occurred.

What Part, If Any, Will the Conferences Play in Assigning Student Grades?

We do not recommend that teachers "grade" student-led conferences. Instead, we suggest that teachers use the student-led conference as an opportunity to help students develop important life skills. As adults, students will be expected to know how to interview for a job, justify a position, set personal and professional goals, and evaluate personal performance. Unfortunately for many students, their first opportunity to apply these skills is in their first job interview or when they apply for a scholarship to a college or university. Student-led conferences provide a relevant, real-world context for students to share their accomplishments, goals, and strategies for improving their performances. Including parents in the student-led conferencing process not only involves them in the child's education and informs them of the child's progress, but also enables students to practice and apply their skills before a caring, supportive audience. For these reasons, we believe that student-led conferences have value far beyond a grade, and, in fact, that grading the child's performance will inhibit some of the other, more significant aspects of the process.

In some districts or states where students are required to meet certain exit outcomes prior to graduation, student-led conferences are an effective strategy for teaching, practicing, and demonstrating progress toward graduation expectations such as becoming an effective communicator, a self-directed learner, and a quality producer. If progress toward such graduation requirements is important to document, the conferences can be used to show that teachers and students are working to meet district and state graduation expectations. But because such expectations usually require a lifetime to master, giving a grade to students for a conference is still inappropriate.

One way that student-led conferences can figure into garnering credit for a class is if the conferences are a requirement for moving on to the next level. In other words, the conference is a prerequisite for getting a grade in the class or receiving a report card. All students must have a conference to complete the class and get the grade they have earned. This method of giving credit for the conferences has proven very successful for students at all levels.

4 Conducting Conferencing

The preparations are done and conference day is here! There is little left to do now but wait for the guests to arrive. One teacher said as she waited expectantly for her parents, "It's like my first party as a teenager. Even though I've sent out the invitations, I'm still afraid nobody will come!" This is exactly how it feels, no matter how many times we have conducted student-led conferences in our own classrooms. We are always a little afraid that the parents won't come—but they do!

What Is the Teacher's Role? Most of the teacher's work is done by the time the conferences arrive, so, except for the nerves that accompany having guests and hoping students will do well, the teacher has it easy during conferences. This is quite a change from the traditional teacher-parent conference where the teacher is in charge and often on the spot! The difference between traditional parent-teacher conferencing and student-led conferencing is due to the shifting of responsibilities from teacher to student, something that has a positive effect on students' attitudes toward learning and that shifts the roles designated to teacher and student in the conferencing process. Because teachers are so used to being in charge, it often feels odd to be an observer rather than an active participant. If the teacher has done a good job preparing students for their conferences, however, then on conference day the teacher can, as we said after our first student-led conferencing experience, enjoy playing host or hostess and entertaining the babies! During student-led conferences, the teacher's role is to do the following things.

Check for Last-Minute Details

Just before parents arrive, teachers may want to do a final check to make sure everything is ready. Welcome signs and any directional signs need to be in place. If conferences are being held in the classroom, student portfolios and conference materials should be easy for students to get them. Parents' information handouts need to be placed near the classroom door close to the conference sign-in sheet so parents and students can pick them up as they sign in for their conference. If the classroom has student desks rather than tables, the desks can be moved together to form clusters. These clusters invite participants to share and discuss work contained in the portfolios. An overhead projector may be set somewhere in the room for students who wish to demonstrate their skills in problem solving, analyzing tests, or organizing information or who are using the overhead to present a lesson or formal presentation to their parents. If a video is going to be shown, the VCR needs to be set up and ready to roll. In addition, the teacher may want to place supplementary resources, such as textbooks, materials, books, and novels, on tables close to the conference areas for students to use as they share their portfolios. Note cards may be placed on the tables for parents to jot down quick observations, thoughts, or reactions during the conference. Be sure student work, displays of three-dimensional models, collections, and artwork throughout the classroom are ready to be shown. Some teachers even go so far as to provide refreshments and flowers and play soft music during the conference, so these would need to be ready for the guests.

Smile and Greet Parents and Guests

As parents and students begin to arrive, the teacher is waiting at the door to greet them warmly and invite them to sign in. For some teachers, this might be the first time that they have met the parents. We have our students practice introducing one adult to another so that they can formally introduce their parents to the teacher if they have not met before. Before parents and students begin the conference, the teacher may want to say a few words of encouragement to the students and to brief parents on what they can expect.

Make Sure Parents Sign in and Get Handout Materials

In the rush to greet parents, introduce them to the teacher, and get the conference started, students may forget to have their parents sign in and take the necessary information sheet. It is important that both of these things happen because the sign-in sheet is the major documentation of who has completed conferences. The information sheet helps the parents be involved in the conferences and requests reflections from them to document how well the conference went. Therefore, one of the teacher's jobs is to be sure that all parents and guests sign in.

Serve as a Student Advocate

Initially, parents may expect the teacher to sit in on the conference as in traditional parent-teacher conferences. The teacher needs to make it very clear from the start that the student is in charge of the conference and that he or she will be available to discuss any questions or concerns at a later time. If the teacher should join the initial stages of the conference, parents will naturally turn to the teacher for explanations and clarification, thus minimizing the effectiveness of the student's role in the conferencing process. Passing the responsibility for explaining and justifying academic progress to the student encourages students to take ownership for their own school performance. If the conference is to be truly meaningful to students, teachers must make a conscious effort to refrain from interfering and let students take charge. Our rule of thumb is never to sit down at the table where the conference is going on; if we do, the student-led conference is over.

Only in rare cases is it appropriate for a teacher to step in and take over a conference, for example, if a young student forgets what to say and becomes increasingly flustered or if a parent becomes domineering or abusive. In the first instance, it is appropriate for the teacher to join the conference by sitting behind the student and coaching him or her through the difficult moment. Once the student has recovered his or her confidence, the teacher can discreetly move away, allowing the student to proceed. In the second instance, the teacher should step in immediately and take over or redirect the conference. Once again, the teacher remains in this role only until the student is able to assume control of the conference. We have never had a conference become so antagonistic that any further action was needed. Having the conferences at school, in the student's environment, seems to have a very positive effect on typical family dynamics and encourages everyone to behave in a civil, adult way—parents as well as students!

Other ways that teachers might act as advocates for students is to help them get materials together if they have forgotten something and take younger children or babies away from the conference so that the students can get the needed attention of the parent or guest. Even in high schools, it is necessary to have an adult monitor for the conferences because the student might need an advocate to help facilitate the process. Sometimes just knowing the teacher is there to assist makes students feel more confident about conducting conferences.

Help Document the Conferencing Process

Documenting the process of the conferences is difficult for several reasons. First, there may be many conferences going on at once, and the teacher will not be an active part of any of them. Second, in many cases, the conference becomes a very personal family communication that one feels shouldn't be scrutinized too closely. It is important, however, that these significant demonstrations of student learning be observed and documented in some way, especially if the conferences are being used to have students demonstrate progress toward district graduation expectations such as effective communication, decision making, and problem solving.

The sign-in sheets can document who had conferences and on what day, and the parent and student reflections will also act as formal, anecdotal documentation of the substance of the conference. The process of the conference, however, must be documented by the neutral observer, the teacher. Teachers should be listening and observing students as they share their class work displayed in the portfolios and interact with their parents and invited guests. If necessary, a teacher could take observation notes on any significant occurrence. A video camera set up in an inconspicuous corner of the classroom is an effective method of documenting the conferences without eavesdropping on the private conversations of the conference participants. If a video camera is not available, teachers can document conferences with snapshots of students and parents examining the portfolios or by taking a "gallery" walk around the classroom, or by students demonstrating their skills on the computer. Later, these photos can be added to portfolios as another form of documentation or as part of the student's postconference reflections.

Parents also need to be reminded to write their child a letter reflecting on the positive aspects of the conference and ways they can help their child with schoolwork. The teacher can refer parents to the parent reflection sheet in the handout packet for help when writing letters. The conference letters are a critical component of the student-led conference. Not only do they provide additional documentation of the conference, they offer parents an opportunity to stress the importance of school and their pride in their child's accomplishments and performance.

Check With Parents to Be Sure They Sign up for an Additional Conference With the Teacher If Needed

As parents prepare to leave, teachers need to find out if parents have any questions. The majority of parents will feel very positive about student-led conferencing, but a few parents may have additional questions or concerns about their child's work or progress. The teacher needs to assure parents that their concerns are very important and that the teacher will be glad to arrange another conference the following week to discuss their concerns.

At the high school level, few parents sign up for additional conferences, but they seem to be reassured that they could if they wanted to. One of the things parents seem to worry about is whether or not simply talking to the child will give them an accurate picture of the student's progress. After conferencing, parents have consistently said that looking at the portfolio and the works in progress folder gave them a much better view of their son or daughter's progress than numbers or letters on a report card. As teachers, we agree with the parents and have found it much easier to talk to parents after student-led conferences because we are all looking at the student work rather than a list of numbers in a grade book.

Another way that parents begin to understand if their child needs some additional help or encouragement to meet the standards required in a course or grade is to see the collected student work that is displayed around the room during conferences. Elementary parents have come to teachers and said, "I noticed that Sally is having trouble reading aloud to me and that her writing isn't as readable as the other work on the bulletin board. What can we do to help her?" This type of parent request will be much more positive in actually getting Sally some help than if the teacher had requested a conference with the parents to alert them to Sally's problem. Because the parents have seen the problem and offered to help, the effort will be collaborative and positive. For the teacher, this is the ideal situation because she or he now has the support of the parents in the effort to improve student performance.

Be Sure Students Say "Thank You" to Guests

Finally, be sure that students give their thank you cards to their guests before they leave. Students could write these cards before the conferences because they know who is coming to meet with them. This can be incorporated into a lesson if writing personal letters is part of the curriculum for that group of students. Students can write individual thank you notes on school stationery or stationery they make in art class, or they can use a form (see p. 135 in Resource A). The teacher also needs to say good-bye to parents and guests and thank them for coming.

In Elementary and Middle School

As the students and parents arrive, students are responsible for introducing their parents or guests to the teacher, finding their portfolios and materials, and inviting their parents to a table to begin the conference.

Once students have finished sharing their portfolios, they will take their parents on a tour or gallery walk of the classroom to explain their daily routines, showing them other student work displayed on bulletin boards and projects too big to be displayed in the portfolio. This tour serves to extend the work represented in the student portfolio and provides parents with a clearer picture of what goes on in the classroom on a daily basis as well as how their child is doing in relation to grade-level expectations.

Students may also have specific demonstrations of their ability to do certain things, lessons they have planned to teach their parents, or presentations they have practiced. If so, they need to be sure they do these before the conferences end. The conferences are concluded when students hand their parents and guests a thank you note for coming to their conference.

In High School

The students should have all the materials for the conference ready to share as well as a script or agenda to make the presentation organized and efficient. As they wait for parents, students can prepare the place where they wish to sit so that the conference will go smoothly. When parents arrive, students should greet them at the door, introduce parents to the teacher, have them sign in, and have them pick up a handout that contains what they should see of student work, and reflection questions they should answer after the conference has concluded. Students should lead their parents or guests to the table and conduct the conference. Students should be prepared to share their notebooks and works in progress folders as well as their portfolios because the work in those collections shows the number and types of assignments students have completed. When these pieces of work are shown with the portfolio, parents get a broad view of the student's performance in class.

Other artifacts of class work can also be shared. Things such as videos of presentations, group work, and discussions can be included along with particular projects and products. Sometimes high school students may prepare demonstrations or lessons for the parents. In classes that have produced videos or products for competitions, these can be available for viewing and explanation. If students are doing a conference that includes more than one content area, they might play a musical piece to show their competence in music, run and discuss a computer program they have created in technology class, do a monologue from a drama class, or conduct some other type of demonstration of what they are learning in various areas of the curriculum.

The major role of the student is to help the parents understand what the student is doing and learning in school, how the student is progressing toward graduation expectations and preparing for his or her adult life, and what the student needs to be working on to improve the quality of his or her work. To do this well, a student must act as the organizer and facilitator of an adult meeting, a role that he or she may never have played before but one that is essential to learn before graduation into the adult work world.

What Is the Parent's Role?

Although the student portfolio is an excellent tool to assess student progress, it is the student-led conference that will motivate students to a higher level of commitment. Giving students an opportunity to share their work with their parents or a significant adult provides a meaningful context for learning and producing quality work. The parent's role in the conferencing process is crucial to the success of the conference.

The first role a parent has is as a listener. The student-led conference provides parents with an opportunity to listen with positive interest to their child as he or she presents the portfolio, discusses his or her strengths and weaknesses as a learner and student, and reviews past goals and establishes new ones for the next marking period. Having an audience for learning gives students a powerful reason to continue to learn and work hard. It validates their school experience by making it real and significant. Listening well is perhaps the most important role of the parents and guests at the conferences.

A second role for parents is to converse with the student about the artifacts in the portfolio and the learning they represent. As parents participate in conversations with their children, they gain a better understanding of not only the academic expectations for their child but what they can do as parents to help and support their child reach his or her academic potential. These discussions between parent and child are beneficial particularly when students are not assuming responsibilities for their schoolwork and a slight "attitude adjustment" is necessary to get students back on track.

Another important role that parents assume in the conferencing process is to help document the conference. At the conclusion of the conference, parents are asked to use the reflection questions in their handout and write a letter to the student about the conference. Later, these letters become part of the student portfolio and are powerful encouragement for students.

In Elementary School

"WELCOME PARENTS, We hope you have a GREAT time at your conference" reads the sign outside a first-grade classroom door greeting parents and students as they enter the classroom and prepare for their student-led conferences.

Students stand nervously as parents sign in and pick up a handout packet. Then, with an audible lump in the throat, the student introductions begin: "Mom, Dad, this is my teacher, Ms. Barnett. Ms. Barnett, this is my mom and dad." After a few words of welcome, students pick up their portfolios and lead their parents to a quiet corner to begin the conference.

As parents follow their children through the classroom toward their seats, they sometimes stop and chat with other parents who are also having conferences. As they settle into their seats, the student explains what he or she will be doing during the conference and then hands the parents the table of contents from the portfolio so that they can follow along with the student presentation of the artifacts.

Various things are going on as students conference with their parents. Some students will present their work samples and reflections from their portfolio as their parents follow along, guided by the table of contents. Others will want to show off new skills by reading to their parents. Looking around the room as conferences take place, it is heartwarming to see parents—mothers and fathers—giving their children undivided attention, leaning forward over small tables to see the work, and asking questions to encourage the children as well as to learn more about what they are sharing.

When the conferences begin to break up and students replace their portfolios on the shelf, parents and students relax. Together, they get a cookie and a drink from the refreshment table set in the corner of the classroom and take a walk around the classroom to look at centers, displays, and projects. As parents and children leave the classroom, parent comments often range from, "You know, I never had to do any of this stuff when I was in school!" to "I never realized how much my child has learned this year!" Sometimes a parent might say, "I know we have some things to work on, but I was really proud of what he (their child) has done these 9 weeks!"

As parents and students alike say good-byes and start out the door, it is impossible to miss the smiles and the fact that the students seem to stand a little taller as they walk down the hall.

In Middle School and High School

The school library is unusually busy as students get their portfolios, works in progress folders, and notebooks out of the crates they used to bring them from the classroom and pick spots for their conferences. Parents will be arriving any minute, and everyone is a little nervous.

When the parents do start coming, students come to the front counter to greet them and introduce them to the teacher. They also ask the parents to sign in and get a handout. As they show their guests to the places where they have set up their agendas, portfolios, and additional materials, students begin to explain how the conferences will go and that the handout tells parents what to look for as well as how to write a reflection on the conference. Most parents take a few minutes to read the handout before the conference begins.

Students who are waiting for their parents are gathered near the door, a little anxious that their parents will forget to come or will be late. Students whose conferences are scheduled for another time, and this is only a few, are working in a corner of the library. They are either getting ready for conferences that will be happening later in the day or doing assignments for this class or other classes. Interestingly, they are not loud and are not paying much attention to the conferences going on in other areas of the library. They obviously have their own work to worry about.

Standing in a corner of the library and looking around, one can easily see the intensity of the conversations going on between students and their parents or guests. One young man is explaining his preface to both parents. Another is showing his guest, his football coach, his works in progress folder to make a point about how much work goes into one assignment. At the next table, a young lady is reading a commentary on a creative artifact aloud to her father, who came from another town for the conference. Nearby, another girl is laughing with her mother as they talk about the student's self-assessment of her work. Most touching of all, one mother is wiping tears as she looks at her son's portfolio. He, by the way, has gone to the teacher to report with dismay that he is embarrassed because his mother is crying! When questioned, it seems he hasn't said anything to upset her. She just started looking at his portfolio and was touched by his evident improvement. Happy tears are not uncommon, even at high school conferences!

At any one time during the day, there are multiple conferences in the library. Sometimes as many as 25 might be going on at once. Even with all the people and activity, the room is remarkably quiet. All the groups are involved in serious discussion, and there is almost no conversation between the separate groups. Students are respectful of other students who are conferencing and do not roam around. Once their own conferences are done, they gather their things, check off their agendas to indicate what they discussed, write their reflections, and join the other students who are not conferencing. All in all, it is quite an impressive and powerful scene to see teenagers talking to their parents for an extended time about their learning. Because many of them may not have had a pleasant or substantive conversation with their parents in some time, the conference offers everyone a positive interaction. Even teenagers who were reluctant to invite their parents to school are enjoying themselves!

Students With Special Needs

What if . . . ?
Variations

Student-led conferences and showcase portfolios offer a wonderful opportunity to celebrate the accomplishments of students with special needs because they provide tangible evidence to parents that their children are learning and making academic progress. Whether the students are in regular classrooms or in self-contained classrooms, these strategies are very powerful opportunities for them to demonstrate their learning and progress. As a parent of a severely learning-disabled child at Union Hill Elementary School remarked after his daughter's student-led conference, "If Misty will put as much effort into her schoolwork as she did into her portfolio and conference, I know she will do well."

The advantages of using student portfolios with special needs children are that they focus on products that show how students have learned to apply processes and skills, they exhibit student work that is judged against the student's last best effort rather than against other students, they allow for modifications needed for some students, and they provide an opportunity to showcase students' individual strengths and special talents. For example, Charlie, a sight-impaired child in the second grade, developed a portfolio of his work using textures and raised letters written in puffy paint. Because Charlie was included in a regular class and would not be able to produce exactly the same type of work the others did, the portfolio allowed the teacher to let Charlie show what he could do in a way appropriate for him. His portfolio was a demonstration of how teachers can differentiate instruction to match student needs. After each grading period, Charlie's parents were able to see the growth he had made from the work samples in his portfolio. At the end of the school year, Charlie's portfolio demonstrated that he had made steady progress in his learning, and his classmates also saw and appreciated all his hard work.

Dennis, a second grader who struggled with reading and writing all year, met with his teacher before his student-led conference to talk about his portfolio and practice for his conference with his parents. As he shared his portfolio selections with his teacher, she was amazed at his ability to recall the skills and strategies he had learned over the past grading period.

For both of these students, the collection in the portfolio and the opportunity to discuss it with a significant adult were rewarding and allowed them to review the content they had studied one more time, something necessary for special needs children.

The positive effect of portfolios for elementary students involved in the Reading Recovery Program in Plano, Texas, has been demonstrated through an 8-year districtwide project to implement portfolios as an alternative assessment in 33 elementary schools. Initially, the district was trying to figure out how to "help the classroom teacher recognize the students as successful learners who had to begin their journeys into literacy at different points" (Haggard, 1998, p. 16). The district researched brain-compatible practices and determined that portfolios combined with various types of conferences with parents would offer a broader picture of what the child was learning and able to apply than standardized tests or averaged grades. According to Haggard (1998), "the [district's] feeling was that with portfolios each child would be evaluated by a set of standards appropriate for his or her stage of development" (p. 15). The program has been a success and removed fear that the portfolios would "water down" the curriculum and student achievement. In fact, students have developed unexpected skills in self-assessment as they have collected and revisited their work and constantly reflected on their learning (Haggard, 1998, p. 16).

Student portfolios combined with student-led conferences provide a better system for documenting student learning and reporting student growth and achievement to special students, their parents, and teachers. As a special education teacher at Atkins Middle School in Winston-Salem, North Carolina, stated, "Having a conference was wonderful for my students. It motivated them to do better work and rewarded them in a positive way. They were doing exactly what all of the other students were doing, being in control of their conferences. Their parents thought it was great!"

Non-Native English-Speaking Students

A growing dilemma in schools is how to manage the increasing number of non-native English-speaking students. Although it may seem that doing portfolios and student-led conferences with these students would be too difficult to make the attempt worthwhile, the strategies have the potential to be an excellent learning experience. Using student-led conferencing also helps to solve a major problem in dealing with non-native speakers, the difficulty of getting these students' parents involved in the school and the child's education.

Often the parents of non-native English speakers do not speak English well either and are intimidated by the school and their child's teacher.

They will not attend school functions because they do not understand the language, and they will not come to conferences with teachers because of the difficulty in communicating. They will, however, attend a student-led conference because their own child is the one extending the invitation and the child will be the one conducting the conference. There is no need for a translator. In fact, the child will be acting as the translator with the teacher.

In schools where there are large populations of non-native English-speaking students, student-led conferencing has proven to be incredibly successful. Fisher Park School is an inner-city school in Ottawa, Ontario, with a large population of immigrant students for whom English is not their first language. Two of the seventh-grade teachers piloted the use of portfolios and student-led conferencing during the 1995-96 school year. After the first conferences, the principal, Bill Langdon, reported,

> They were awesome! The normal parent teacher interview turnout for our regular English program is about 20% and the French Immersion program is about 80%. The student-led parent conferences have a 90% attendance rate!! Interviews took place in several of our many languages. Parents who had never previously visited the school responded to their child's invitation. This validates our earlier impression that this style of conference had enormous power for the multicultural school. This aspect surpassed my expectations. (personal communication, December 5, 1995)

We have seen equally remarkable success with non-native English-speaking students in other schools where we have facilitated the use of portfolios and student-led conferencing. We recommend that teachers use these strategies with such students, because they can create portfolios and have quality conferences with their parents and benefit in all the same ways other students do. We need to do all we can to encourage them to communicate effectively and to get their parents involved in their education; student-led conferencing can be a marvelous tool to do both.

Home Conferences

In some elementary schools, the second conference of the school year is held at home. Students prepare for these conferences in exactly the same way they do for the school conferences. The only difference is that they take their portfolios home to share them with their parents. The advantage of having a home conference is that it offers members of the family who ordinarily do not or cannot attend a parent-teacher conference an opportunity to see what the child is doing in school and share in his or her academic successes. We found that the participation of fathers at the spring student-led conferences drastically improves after home conferences in the winter. Perhaps it is because they have a better idea of how important and enjoyable the conferences can be! Home conferences can also be an excellent way of conducting conferences with severely disabled students who have not been mainstreamed into the classroom and with students who are homebound.

At the middle school and high school levels, home conferences are, as a rule, not very successful. If the conference is required to complete the school year or a particular course, it is hard to hold the students accountable for having a conference when we cannot control the situations at home that might prevent students from conducting a conference. Our students have reported that it is often hard to get the full attention of parents when the phone is ringing, the TV is on, younger brothers and sisters are present, dinner has to be fixed, and so on. It is also not always easy for parents to exchange roles and allow the child to take the lead in the discussion. As one 16-year-old reported, "It was Mama's table, and I couldn't get a word in once we started."

Despite the fact that home conferences are not as productive or controllable as conferences at school, sometimes it is necessary to have conferences at home for students who are ill or for parents who cannot attend but want to be part of the process their children are going through. If a home conference is needed for secondary students, they should be required to prepare just as they would for a school conference. They should also write a narrative of what occurred in the conference to accompany their conference reflection. This narrative should include when and where the conference occurred, how long it was, and the sequence of items discussed. The parents can be asked to sign the student's agenda and write a reflection to help document the conference. The teacher will need to set a target date by which time the conference must have taken place and collect the student's narrative and reflections along with the parent reflection to document the conference.

Team, Grade-Level, or Schoolwide Conferencing

South Fork Elementary School—Grade Level

At South Forth Elementary School, a large elementary school of 1,000 students in Winston-Salem, North Carolina, the second-grade teachers began implementing portfolios and student-led conferencing after attending a conference conducted by us. Seven teachers attended the conference; since then, another teacher has joined the team from a school that was already using portfolio assessment.

Although the teachers at South Fork are using basically the same system as described in this book, each teacher has a different process for collecting and selecting portfolio samples. Some teachers have students select work samples for their portfolios throughout the grading period, other teachers have their students choose papers that represent quality work only, and still others have students select work from the works in progress folders 2 weeks before conferences. Teachers use different containers for portfolios. Some use two-pocket folders, and others have manila folders decorated by the students.

The teachers report that the greatest challenge of working in a large team is that not all teachers received their training at the same time. Some were trained in a 2-day summer workshop, and others were trained by their colleagues who attended the workshop. It took 2 years to get every teacher on the team convinced to try the methods with students. Once everyone had lived the experience, however, they were able to see the benefits of portfolios and student-led conferencing for their students and parents. Now everyone is committed to making these practices part of their routine. They are setting the dates for next year's conferences and making plans to improve the process.

Union Hill Elementary School—Whole School

Union Hill Elementary School in High Point, North Carolina, has many of the same problems that plague inner-city schools throughout the country. At the end of the 1996-97 school year, Union Hill was designated as low performing by the state, and the teachers knew they could not raise student performance without the help of parents who rarely came to school functions. The teachers were desperate to find ways to get parents more involved in what their children were doing at school. As one teacher remarked, "The only time our parents come is when we feed them."

Teachers introduced their students to the idea of student-led conferencing after attending several workshops. Over the course of the next few months, teachers and students worked to create their portfolios and prepare for their conferences. Some teachers were very excited about the concept of student-led conferences. Others were less than enthusiastic, but all agreed to try it one time.

The evening of March 19 was designated as conference night. Two weeks before, the entire school kicked into gear to get ready. Teachers shared ideas, brainstormed solutions to problems, and adapted the student-led conferencing process to fit the abilities of their students. John Pruette, the pre-kindergarten teacher, gave new meaning to the term *student-led.* He decided that his little ones would take their parents around to each center in the classroom and together they would complete an activity.

The day before the conferences, every classroom was a flurry of activity. Everywhere students were putting the finishing touches on their portfolios and practicing for their conferences. The teachers looked a bit frenzied, but ready for the next evening's visitors.

Finally, conference night came and everything was ready. At 5:45, one of the PTA officers leaned over and said, "They (the parents) won't come, they only come when we have food." At 6:00, however, cars began to arrive, and by 6:30 both parking lots were full and parents were parking on the road. They came! Moms and dads, grammas and grandpas, brothers and sisters came to school to share in the conferences the students were conducting.

Walking down the hall, it was hard to miss the excitement in the teachers' voices. For teachers who had spent a year hearing about their low-performing school from the state, the local press, and their district administrators, this night was a victory. A fifth-grade teacher said, "This is great! Tonight I am really proud to be a teacher!"

That night 76% of the students at Union Hill Elementary School were represented by one or more parent or guest. The teachers who had been excited about the process and had made an effort to contact parents personally had close to 100% parent attendance. Those who tried to pull everything together at the last minute and sent a quick note right before conference night to inform parents were disappointed in their parent turnout. The message was clear that to have a successful schoolwide conferencing night, everyone needed to be planning for it well in advance and parents needed to be informed and contacted early and often.

In her "Good Morning Note" to her teachers, Susan Britt, the principal (March 20, 1998), made the following statement:

> Congratulations on the wonderful performance of your students last night! I was completely bowled over by the number of parents who participated. No one can ever say again that our parents don't care about their kids or that they don't show up for them. Last night's event is one of the first really concrete evidences that we are no longer a low-performing school. (See p. 138 in Resource A.)

Everyone was amazed at the success of the student-led conference night. Teachers had never seen so many parents at the school enjoying their children's achievements. Their experience proved once again what we have often said to teachers in training sessions, to take a line from *Field of Dreams,* "If you build it, they will come!" One teaching assistant echoed what many felt at Union Hill when she was overheard saying as she walked down the hall, "They came and we didn't even have to feed them!"

Atkins Middle School—Grade Level

The eighth-grade teachers at Atkins Middle School in Winston-Salem, North Carolina, were trained in the summer of 1997 and implemented one student-led conference for all 251 eighth-grade students on April 7, 1998. They scheduled conferences during the school day from 7:00 a.m. until 4:00 p.m. On that day, 210 parents came for the conferences, and most other students had conferences with invited guests. Some of the guests were invited by the principal, Debbie Blanton, to be on hand for students who needed someone to conference with them. These guests were school board members, parents from the school parent support organization, representatives of the school's business partners, and folks from the district central office, including one of the assistant superintendents. During a makeup day the following week, all the students who were absent on the conference day had conferences with their parents or with adults within the school.

The teachers were so excited about the success of their first conferences that they planned two for the next year, and the sixth- and seventh-grade teachers attended training sessions during the summer so that all students in the school could have portfolios and conferences during the 1998-99 school year. The principal proposed that the school apply for a waiver from the district to have conferences during the school day on the day before the systemwide scheduled conference day in the fall. The school would be open for conferences from 7:00 a.m. until 7:00 p.m. to accommodate the working schedules of parents so that more of them could attend. The following day, with the students out of school for the traditional teacher-parent conferences, faculty would have a compensation day off because they had worked a long day the day before.

Some of the organizational strategies that this school used to hold grade-level conferences were:

- To have one teacher appointed as the coordinator to work out the scheduling of conferences
- To mail formal invitations to all parents and follow up with phone calls if response cards were not returned
- To inform parents that all students had to have a conference to complete the requirements for eighth grade
- To have students prepare for their conferences by writing an agenda and practicing a 15-minute conference with seventh-grade students who were prepared with questions to ask about the work in the portfolios

- To hold most of the conferences in the school's library, using vacant classrooms at times when there were a large number of conferences scheduled during the same hour
- To have student guides to show parents where the conferences were being held
- To ask parents to reflect on the back of the information handout and leave the reflection sheets with the teacher on duty in the room where they had the conference
- To take pictures of the conferences between students and school board members, business partners, and district office staff and send these with thank you notes from the principal for attending the conferences
- To use a form for students to write thank you cards to give parents and guests as they left
- To work together to be sure that students were doing reflection, to coordinate what should be in the portfolio, to plan for putting the portfolios together and prepare for conferences so no single teacher or content area was overburdened

During their debriefing after the conferences, teachers shared many evidences of the success of the portfolios and conferences. They were particularly pleased and surprised at the way that the conferences had gone between students and guests who were not their parents. They relayed one case of a guest who was impressed with a young man's social studies project on World War II, where he had interviewed veterans and gotten so excited about the period that he had gone on and done additional research on the military. The young man was not a particularly good student and had gotten some needed praise from his guest, someone who was not influenced by his previous school performance. Another guest of a student whose parents were not interested in coming was so delighted with the conference that she wrote a note to the parents thanking them for letting her meet with their son, of whom they must be especially proud. The guest had no idea about the situation, but did exactly the right thing to enhance the young man's self-esteem and point out that the parents' disinterest had caused them to miss something special with their son.

The teachers spent most of their debriefing time celebrating the success of the conferences, but they thought about how they could improve them next year. They wisely realized that they would need to continue the monthly meetings they held throughout the year to discuss and coordinate their portfolio and conferencing processes. They recorded their ideas for improving conferences the next year so they would not forget them and planned to gather at the end of the school year to look over the parent and student reflections together.

Floresville Middle School—Whole School

Floresville Middle School is in a rural community in south Texas. Teachers began using portfolios and student-led conferencing during a summer school session in 1996. The strategies were so successful that in the following school year, all the eighth-grade students did one student-led conference in the spring. During the 1997-98 school year, every student at Floresville Middle School did two student-led conferences—one in the fall and one in the spring.

In their 2-year experience with portfolios and conferencing, Floresville teachers improved their process each time. Some of the strategies they used to facilitate whole school conferencing included the following:

- Having a meeting in September to select the dates for the conferences
- Assigning teachers who had done conferencing before to be mentors to those for whom the process would be new
- Notifying students through language arts classes in September that they would be having conferences
- Showing students sample student portfolios
- Starting works in progress folders in all classes
- Informing parents about the student-led conferences at the open house in September
- Giving every teacher a memo with a timeline for preparing for conferences and specific duties that the teacher needed to carry out to facilitate the process
- Staggering the conferences so that the eighth grade had them on one day and the seventh grade had them on the following day
- Mailing invitations in the form of a letter from the principal explaining the conferencing process and rationale to parents 2 weeks before the conferences
- Calling parents 5 days before conferences if they had not returned response cards
- Having students decorate manila folders for their portfolios and select one to two pieces of work from each class
- Ensuring that students had done self- and peer assessments on their portfolios before the conferences
- Asking parents to report to the office for directions to the conference area designated for their child
- Calling students out of class to join their parents in the school library or other location
- Arranging for paraprofessionals to check parents in and call students so that there was a record of who had conferenced that day
- Having teachers monitor conferences during their planning periods and after school

- Making sure that all students had a conference within the conferencing week

Teachers at Floresville report that the conferences have improved the quality of student work by raising the level of concern due to the fact that it will be viewed by someone other than the classroom teacher. It has also served as another way to encourage the parent-teacher partnership which is so crucial to education (L. Lucio & D. Porter, personal communication, February 24, 1998).

East Forsyth High School—Grade Level

East Forsyth High School in Winston-Salem, North Carolina, began using portfolios and student-led conferencing as a major part of its ninth-grade Quality Academy in the fall of 1996. Teachers received 2 days of training and had formal follow-up and support sessions with the trainer throughout the next 2 years. This high school is in a fast-growing area just beyond the city limits of one of the larger cities in North Carolina. The school serves approximately 1,550 students, most coming from middle-class families. The Quality Academy was intended to address severe problems with ninth-grade discipline, dropouts, and low academic performance as well as prepare these students for new, more demanding district graduation requirements going into effect for the class of 2000. The Quality Academy has been extremely successful, exceeding expectations for improving ninth graders' behavior and academic success (see Chapter 6 for statistics).

To accomplish the implementation of portfolios and conferencing in a large high school, the ninth-grade teachers used numerous logistical strategies and met together at crucial times to adjust the process to meet their situation. Some of the tactics they employed included the following:

- Determining what needed to be done to organize portfolios and prepare for conferences
- Designating certain content areas to carry out the duties (e.g., math teachers had students create the covers for their portfolios and helped them write agendas for conferences, language arts teachers had students write prefaces for their portfolios and facilitated the student self-assessment, social studies teachers provided the portfolio binders and the conferences were conducted during social studies classes, and science teachers had students practice for their conferences and facilitated the peer assessment of portfolios)
- Having the school purchase binders for every ninth-grade student to ensure that they would all have one as well as giving each student a binder to create a high school portfolio that would eventually

have artifacts from each of the 4 years (These binders were paid for by a business partner of the school, and the following year a new set of binders in a different color were purchased for the incoming freshman class. Students are doing one student-led conference at the end of 10th grade for which they added to the ninth-grade portfolio. They will continue to add to the portfolio in 11th and 12th grade, but instead of conferences, they will be doing formal presentations to evaluation committees.)

- Setting up a schedule for the process (The timeline specifies dates for getting necessary tasks done. The tasks listed on the schedule are sending out invitations, creating a class rubric stating each subject's criteria and standards for portfolio entries, collecting student work, making selections and writing commentaries, assembling the portfolios, doing self- and peer assessment of portfolios, creating an agenda for the conferences, practicing a conference, and conducting conferences.)

- Meeting in content area groups to discuss what entries should be in the portfolios for each subject

- Setting aside a portfolio day several days before the conferences were scheduled to get the whole collection together (On this day, students picked up their binders from the social studies teachers and carried them around all day to put in the entries from each class they attended. At the end of the day, students left their portfolios in their last class. The spine of each portfolio binder had the social studies teacher's name on it so teachers could sort and return them to the proper teacher.)

- Creating a formal invitation that included a restatement of the reasons why the school was requiring that students keep portfolios and conduct conferences (These invitations were mailed to parents in envelopes without any school logo or address to increase the likelihood they would get to parents and not be intercepted by students who might think they were some sort of discipline or poor grade notice.)

- Inviting community members, business partners, and district administrators to join them for conference day

- Starting conferences at least 1/2 hour after the beginning of the school day to avoid a major traffic problem as students were arriving for school

- Having at least one teacher monitoring conferencing areas at all times

- Offering evening conferencing time as well as during the school day for parents who could not leave work for conferences

- Having most conferences in the school library but using vacant classrooms if needed
- Making directional signs for parents to get to classrooms to pick up their children for conferences
- Creating a parent handout containing the purposes of conferences, the required contents for portfolios, prompts to use to help students conference well, and reflection questions with space for the parents to write comments
- Collecting parent reflections as parents left the conference
- Taking time in the following day's social studies classes to have students do oral reflection on the conferences
- Setting a deadline for all students to have conferences completed

One of the interesting things that the East Forsyth teachers discovered was that they had to be especially careful during the second year to be sure that they did all the necessary things for conferences to be successful. For example, they had to be as careful as they were the first year to inform parents well about what the school was doing and why. Because they had gotten a lot of positive publicity in the community the first year, they assumed parents would know what conferences were and why they were important. They forgot that the incoming ninth graders and their parents might never have heard about portfolios and student-led conferencing. The first conferences of the second year were not as well attended as the previous year, and in a problem-solving session, the teachers discovered that they had not informed the parents or the students well. Because neither students nor parents really understood why they were doing the conferences and what benefits students would gain from the experience, few students conducted quality conferences and fewer parents than expected came. Once they realized the problem, teachers addressed the situation, and the spring conferences went very well.

Another area that teachers worked to improve during the second year was the quality of the portfolios. They discovered that they needed to talk to each other to ensure that every teacher was in fact having students save work and select entries for the portfolios. They also had to work harder to be sure that the entries gave a complete picture of the curriculum required in individual courses. It was important that students discuss their learning in relation to the state-mandated curriculum and that the artifacts in the portfolios were evidence of the student's progress toward graduation requirements. In a high school setting where students may have as many as seven classes a day, creating a collection of learning artifacts that is balanced among all courses and of consistently high quality is very difficult. There must be a lot of conversation and coordination between all teachers involved and strong leadership and support from administrators. East Forsyth's ninth-grade Quality Academy teachers have been and are continuing to work to solve the logistical problems associated with using showcase portfolios in student-led conferencing in a secondary school.

Rideau High School—Whole School

At Rideau High School in Ottawa, Ontario, student-led conferencing began in the ninth grade after a cross-curricular team of teachers attended a training session in the fall of 1995. During school year 1996-97, the conferencing was done in all 9th- and 10th-grade classes because of the success of the previous year's 9th-grade efforts. By the next school year, students from all grades, 9 through 13, were conducting conferences using their portfolios as evidence of their learning. These conferences occurred in December and April and replaced the school's traditional parent-teacher interviews (Rideau High School's Portfolio Committee, 1997).

Orchestrating a schoolwide effort in portfolios and conferencing takes planning and perseverance. Rideau High School's method of implementation included the following steps (P. McCahill & J. Robson, personal communication, February 14, 1998):

- Planning a publicity strategy before the start of the school year so parents would be well informed early and could anticipate the conferences
- Establishing a Portfolio Committee and appointing one teacher member as coordinator for the portfolio and conferencing effort
- Creating a handbook for teachers that included timelines, rationale, advice, sample materials, and master copies used to inform parents and students and then spending staff development time at the beginning of the year reviewing and discussing it
- Training teachers in how to create their own professional portfolios and encouraging them to begin
- Having students who had experience in conducting student-led conferences talk to teachers and other students who were new at it
- Giving parents information about the upcoming conferences in the beginning-of-the-year parents' night meetings
- Keeping works in progress folders in each subject area classroom
- Planning conferences three quarters of the way through each semester so that students still had time to improve their academic performances before final marks were given
- Sending parents invitations that specified appointment times and following up with phone calls to determine who would be conferencing with the students
- Having a student assembly 4 days before conferences where staff modeled conferences by playing the role of students in different situations, for example, the student with a perfect portfolio, the

student with an average portfolio, and the student with an empty portfolio

- Putting portfolios together in the presentation areas on the day of the conferencing and requiring students to sign out portfolios for conferences and return them after
- Assigning staff members to monitor presentation areas—the school cafeteria, library, and gym—and be available to speak to parents and students after the conferences (Teachers were given specific instructions not to intervene in conferences.)
- Having large posters for parents to sign and comment on conferences before leaving
- Having students write reflective essays on the conferences and share them in informal class discussions
- Having the staff reflect through a survey after the second conferences of the year

Like the East Forsyth teachers, Rideau High School teachers struggled with the issue of quality in the student portfolios. They addressed this by implementing several practices. First, they established the criteria for the portfolios in rubrics or checklists that take into account such things as completeness, care and quality, reflective essays, and student effort to edit and correct work that had been previously evaluated. The portfolios were compulsory and counted as 10% to 15% of the term mark. Approximately 50% of the entries in the portfolios were required by the teachers, and the rest were student selected. Portfolio content (Rideau High School Portfolio Committee, 1998) was shaped to reflect the 10 essential learning outcomes from the Ontario Common Curriculum, employability skills, and student ability in the multiple intelligences. The teachers also discovered portfolios were better if students were required to edit and correct assignments as they were completed, write the reflections on pieces soon after they had completed them, and file the assignments and reflections until it was time to compile the portfolio.

In all these schools, the teachers have taken the basic processes for having students construct showcase portfolios and conduct conferences and adapted them to their own situations. In many cases, their adaptations improved on the original way that we used portfolios and conferencing in our classrooms. We have learned a great deal by working with these teachers, and we are grateful to them for their dedication and generosity in sharing their experiences and good ideas for making these strategies work on the larger scale of grade levels and schools.

Reflecting and Celebrating 5

When you hear a student say, "Doing a portfolio has taught me a lot about presenting my work in the best way I can," you know something incredible has taken place. The day after the conferences is always reserved for reflection. Reflection is the last component in the student-led conferencing process and undoubtedly one of the most important. Taking time to look back over the process and the events leading up to the student-led conference is time well spent for all involved. Parents and guests need to document their responses to students, to record how impressed they were. Students benefit from reflection because it makes them "linger over their learning" one last time. They also need to set goals and select strategies for improving their performance for the next time. Teachers benefit from reflection because it makes them stop, take a "breather" and think about their teaching before charging into the next book or unit of instruction. Teachers will have the added advantage of being able to take into account the parent and student reflections in their own analyses. This is important because it is in the reflection and assessment of the process that teachers problem solve and determine how to make the process even more efficient and effective the next time they facilitate portfolio development and conferences. In an activity as complex as this one, reflection after the fact is essential in getting down all the emotions, benefits, and areas for improvement.

Parent Reflection

Parent reflections are the icing on the cake. When a teacher was asked, "What part of the student-led process do you like the best?" she remarked, "Watching the students conduct their conferences and take ownership of their process." Then she added, "The parent reflections make you feel good!" Schools ask for parent feedback in many different ways, but the important thing is to have some form of written reflection from parents.

If a school has a giant book, or a large poster board for parents to put comments on as they leave, the comments will be brief. Some samples from Floresville Middle School indicate the type of immediate responses parents offer:

"Great idea. Made the kids really think about quality."

"I really enjoyed my daughter's presentation. The one-on-one is a great concept."

"I'm glad we were given this time at school with our child."

"I was happy to see Ryan is becoming organized. I think this type of activity encourages focus on goals for the future."

"I enjoy and appreciate the opportunity to view John's work so that I can make suggestions during the year that will be of benefit to my son."

If a school is asking parents to write letters to the students, the reflections will be more personal and elaborate. This type of response from the parents or guests is more useful to the student. In fact, students treasure these letters, and they become an important addition to the portfolios. Some sample quotes point out the power of these reflections to enhance student self-esteem:

"I am very proud of the work displayed in your portfolio. It's a wide variety and gives a good overall view of the things you're covering in class. I was impressed with the thoroughness that is shown so that I, as a parent, am made aware of your daily progress as well as the extended projects." (mother of a special needs high school student, March 31, 1994)

"I didn't realize how scared and nervous you are about high school. Don't worry . . . Dad and I are behind you 100%." (parents of a middle school student, April 16, 1997)

"I see the improvement in your work. I see where you are learning that practice, persistence, and patience do pay off. I also noted that in some areas your handwriting even was NEAT! GREAT! Keep trying—I'm proud of you." (mother of an elementary student, December 14, 1992)

The parent reflection letters also provide teachers with valuable feedback about how parents feel about the student-led conferences. One parent of a kindergarten student attached a note to her letter to him. It read,

P.S. Ms. Donahue and Ms. Nobel, Portfolio Night is a great idea! It was a great way to see what your child is really doing in school. It also lets your child know that you really care about them and what they're doing and learning.

The mother of an early elementary student wrote an extra letter to her daughter's teacher saying,

> I have thoroughly enjoyed the student-led conferences and portfolios. The letters on a report card are very subjective. With the portfolio, I see Christy's pride and ownership. She is becoming the responsible party. She enjoys taking charge of her learning, and I hope she will continue.

Perhaps the highest complement a parent can pay is to see the value of the instructional and assessment methods and begin to use them. The following comment from the mother of a high school student came as a surprise, but reinforced everything students were doing with their portfolios. She wrote to the teacher,

> In watching Kelly spend time organizing her work, reflecting on it, choosing what best exemplifies her growth, etc. I decided I should do the same. Here in the second year of my doctoral studies, I have begun my own portfolio. It has been fun to gather these materials and has been a wonderful morale booster when I think I'm not getting anywhere.

One mother showed her support for the student-led conferences over the traditional parent-teacher conferences by writing in her letter to her fourth-grade son, "I enjoyed your conference the most. Don't tell your brothers."

Parent comments are also needed to find out how teachers can make the experience even more meaningful. At East Forsyth High School, it was parent comments to the effect that they didn't really see why they came to school for conferences that clued teachers into the fact that they had not informed parents as well as they needed to or prepared students to have quality, substantive conferences. Because of this feedback, the teachers were able to address the problems and drastically improve the conferences the next time.

Student Reflection

Reflecting the day after the student-led conference is natural for students whose teacher has built reflection into the daily routine (see p. 136 in Resource A). Student reflections in the early grades often focus on the event itself: Who came, what did you do, how did it go? The responses are overwhelmingly positive from even the youngest students. As one first grader at Mabel Elementary wrote in her postconference reflection, "I loved it. Shode my kite, my hart, and my 3 leaf clover!" Antonio, a first grader from Union Hill Elementary, wrote, "I like my confernce last nite. I read my portf and I talk about my doing words book." Often the postconference reflection for little ones is done orally in whole class discussion. Teachers can record this type of reflection on video. In such a session, one second grader remarked that he liked these conferences better than the ones the previous year because he was in charge instead of the teacher, and he was the one who knew what he had learned anyway!

Fifth-grade students at Crichton Alternative Community Public School in Ottawa, Ontario, agreed when they wrote about the differences between student-led conferences and parent-teacher interviews. They said things like, "I'm part of my SLC [student-led conference], but I've never been a part of a parent-teacher interview," "You are leading the conference instead of the teacher leading the conference," and "Your parents get to hear how you feel about your work" (Roberts, 1996, p. 5). For all students, being the one in charge of the conference is a positive experience. Even students who do not have much quality work to share can explain what they are learning and where they are in the process of achieving the academic level they are expected to reach.

Student reflection in the intermediate, middle, or high school may concentrate on what the students did during the conference and learned from the process. As an intermediate student wrote, "I have learned to organize my work, set up my work in a portfolio, and present it to my parents, and present it in an orderly fashion" (Roberts, 1996, p. 1). A high school senior reflected,

> I learned that I need to straighten my act up and be more organized with my work. I've learned to stand back and take a look at my work and see if it is quality work. . . . I've learned it will take a lot of time to produce quality work, and you have to be willing to put forth the effort to get it.

The life lessons evident in this reflection are what we all hope students will take away from the experience of school along with the content knowledge from courses.

In all cases, students need to look at what they can do the next time they hold conferences to improve their performances. It is this self-analysis during the reflection process that enables students to set goals for future improvement and motivates them to become self-directed learners. At the first conference in the fall, such reflection should focus on preparing to do even better at the second conference. At the end of the year, students are often looking ahead to how they can use the skills beyond the current classroom. A fourth-grade student reflecting on what he had gained from doing the conferences said, "It can make me be less nervous about being interviewed for a job, or meeting with my boss" (Roberts, 1996). We are not always aware of just how far students are looking ahead and how much they understand about what we are teaching unless we ask them! In her postconference reflection, a senior high school student remarked, "Now that my portfolio is complete, I feel it shows a lot about the person I am, what is important to me, and all of my dreams. I really am proud of my portfolio, and I want to save it to read in the future and see how many goals I have reached."

Don't skip the time for students to reflect on the process of the conferences and their final portfolios! It is here that teachers find out if they taught well because students will let them know what they are taking away from the experience of being in class. Students need time to linger over the learning, and teachers need to hear what students have to say.

Teacher Reflection

Once the conferences are over, most teachers need time to step back and reflect over the events leading up to and including the student-led conferences (see p. 137 in Resource A). The impressions that stay freshest in our minds are the dramatic ones, the ones that catch our hearts. These are the memories that motivate teachers to continue using portfolios and student-led conferencing even though both involve a lot of work. One afternoon, J. Shoemaker, a first-year elementary teacher, was standing in her doorway waiting for parents to arrive for student-led conferences and relaying how one of her students said earlier that day that her mother was not coming for her conference. Apparently the child's mother never comes to anything at school. Overhearing the little girl's statement, her friend, Margie, said, "That's OK. My mom can conference with both of us." The teacher reflected later that Margie's mother brought both girls back to school and completed a student-led conference with each one. Shoemaker wrote, "It was a fantastic night! I hope that we continue this in the future. I was overwhelmed by emotion the whole night, it was incredible" (personal communication, March 19, 1998).

Many teachers may recall times during the conferences that they over-heard students explaining concepts to their parents that the teachers had no idea they had remembered. C. Stone, a third-grade teacher, comments,

> I didn't realize how much my students knew. When I ask the kids to review what they have learned in class, they say, "Huh?" But, at the conference I heard them telling their parents about every-thing we had done in class. (personal communication, March 19, 1998)

Another teacher reports, "I heard one student say, 'This is a timeline and it tells you how much time has lapsed between events'" (S. Keely, personal communication, March 19, 1998).

Sometimes a disappointing turnout can turn into a learning experi-ence. One teacher reflects, after having a low parent turnout at her student-led conferences compared with her colleagues, "I had 12 very disappointed students this morning and 10 whose toes were off the ground." Asked what she would have done differently, she replied that she should have contacted parents earlier and also said, "I would have begun assembling the portfolios 2 weeks earlier and had them completed

1 week prior to the conferences. Too much last-minute rushing around. My fault! I made myself crazy. It will be more fun next time."

When teachers reflect on the overall benefits of doing student-led conferences, their hearts are on their sleeves because the experience is so powerful for them, their students, and the parents and guests. As L. Lucio writes,

> The experience [of student-led conferencing] also provides time for parents and children to spend "quality time" together discussing quality work. Parents now have an opportunity to visit the school to participate in a positive, non-threatening activity. (personal communication, February 24, 1998)

When asked about the effect that student-led conferencing had had on her parents and students, D. Sheedy, a first- and second-grade teacher from Batesville, Texas, responded,

> These conferences have helped parents stay informed on how their child is doing. It has made the parents aware of any problems which their child may be having, so they can be helped. It has also helped me maintain a better working condition with my students because they know their parents will see the work. (personal communication, March 3, 1998)

It is moving to see parents and students interacting in positive ways, and it is rewarding to have been the one who helped make that happen.

Celebration for All   We wanted to be sure to include this aspect of the conferencing experience so that teachers would not forget to enjoy and reward themselves and students by taking some time to celebrate the whole event. Comments from guests, observers, and administrators can act as recognition and reward for the successful completion of a conferencing event (see p. 138 in Resource A). The reflections are part of the celebration because they allow everyone to relive the high spots, and there are many! As Floresville Middle School teachers were debriefing their experiences in their first student-led conferences, the facilitator asked each teacher to share a positive aspect of the portfolios and conferencing and to provide one example to support what he or she felt was successful. The 10 teachers and principal shared successes for more than an hour and a half, and everyone in the room was immensely touched by what they had accomplished for their students. The session ended with some emotional tears, smiles, and hugs. It was the kind of celebration we rarely allow ourselves, but need to have more often.

Students need to celebrate also. The conferences are a form of celebration and often feel very festive, but there needs to be some sort of "high five" for the kids once the job is done. They will be energized and

Improving Student Learning 6

The Evidence

Yes! The evidence that these two strategies work to improve student learning is mounting. Both statistical evidence and more qualitative, anecdotal evidence are being gathered in the classrooms and schools using student showcase portfolios in conferencing. The statistics that show student gains in performance on local and state tests are convincing and sometimes dramatic, but we must admit to being more moved by the personal reflections and success stories coming from classrooms.

Is There Evidence That Student-Led Conferencing Using Showcase Portfolios Improves Student Learning?

Improvement in High School

One school that has been keeping a record of the effect of these strategies is East Forsyth High School in Kearnersville, North Carolina. This high school of approximately 1,550 students is located in one of the fastest growing areas in central North Carolina. In the 1996-97 school year, Dr. Judy Grissom, principal, began an initiative called the Quality Academy for ninth graders. This effort was intended to help ninth graders adjust to high school, lower the student dropout rate, and begin to prepare these students of the class of 2000 for new and more rigorous graduation standards in the Winston-Salem/Forsyth school district. The centerpiece of the program is the use of student showcase portfolios and two student-led conferences during the school year. During the 1995-96 school year, Dr. Grissom kept data about the performance of the freshman class. These data include the percentage of the school's dropouts who were ninth graders and the percentage of ninth-grade students failing two or more classes (see Figure 6.1).

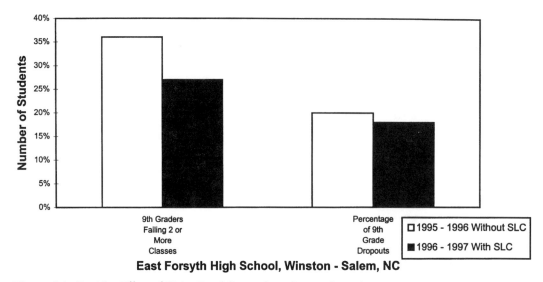

Figure 6.1. Positive Effect of Using Portfolios and Student-Led Conferencing in High School

Data collected 1 year after the program began indicate that the program was very successful. Not only were grades up, but discipline referrals and students sent to alternative schools for discipline problems were down despite the fact that the class of 1996-97 was larger than the previous freshman class (see Figure 6.2). Anyone who is familiar with high school students can appreciate that such a dramatic improvement in student behavior is remarkable and would make it easier for all students to learn more content.

According to Dr. Grissom, another area of success has been parent participation. Parent attendance at the conferences has ranged from 82% to 75% (Grissom, 1997), a much higher rate than parent participation in other school functions, and certainly higher than the traditional open house night at a high school. This kind of increase in parent participation in school conferences has also been noted at Rideau High School in Ottawa, Ontario. According to John Robson, head of social sciences and coordinator of the portfolio committee,

> prior to student-led conferences, only about 10% of parents came to traditional parent-teacher interviews. In our first conference (with ninth graders only), we had 96% attendance, and in our most recent conferences (which included students in the entire school grades 9-13) we had 80% participation from parents. (personal communication, February 14, 1998)

Mr. Robson also reports that the quality of student work was superior when students knew that someone other than their teacher would be

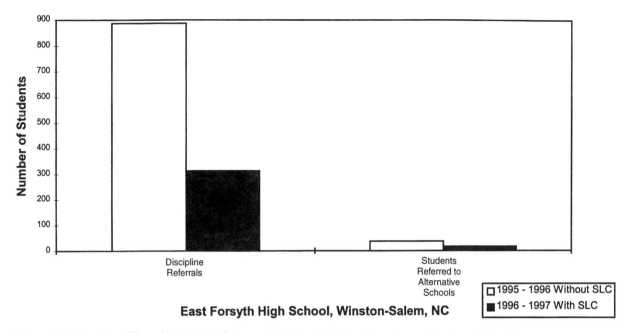

Figure 6.2. Positive Effect of Using Portfolios and Student-Led Conferencing on Students' Behavior

looking at it, and students put extra effort into the organization and aesthetics of their portfolios.

East Forsyth High School's success has been so remarkable that it is now getting attention from the community and other schools in its district and state. It was awarded the 1997-98 Governor's Programs of Excellence in Education Award for its Quality Academy. Its example has also convinced Atkins Middle School, one of the middle schools that sends students to East, to began using portfolios and conferencing.

Improvement in Middle School

Another school with totally different demographics has had equally dramatic results. Floresville Middle School in Floresville, Texas, began using portfolios and student-led conferencing as the major assessment piece in a summer academy in June 1996. This was an attempt to help students who had not passed their state tests and could not go on to the next grade level without summer remediation. The teachers involved in the summer program decided that just doing more of the same was not going to be successful with these students and that they wanted to do whatever was necessary to give these students the tools they needed to succeed, not only in summer school but also in the next school year. They worked together to connect the curriculum in relevant ways for students, and had students create showcase portfolios and conduct conferences at the end of the session. According to the teachers who signed parents in,

80% of the students had one or more family member attend the conferences. The other 20% conferenced with adult guests other than their parents. In their team reflections, these teachers stated, "We were surprised and pleased with the pride, seriousness, and, in some cases, joy that these students demonstrated in relating and explaining their accomplishments. Parent comments were also very gratifying" (G. Johnston, N. Tackitt, & G. Gleeson, personal communication, August 16, 1996). Some sample comments from parents that appeared in a local newspaper article about the Summer Achievement Academy confirm the teacher's comments. One parent responded, "I believe that if you can keep a student interested, he'll learn, and my child is learning!" Another expressed appreciation at being part of the child's learning by saying, "Thanks for allowing me to come and evaluate my child's portfolio. This is another great way for parents to get involved!" ("Floresville Achievement Academy Graduates First Class," July 24, 1996).

The effect of the successful summer was felt through the whole school the following year. In April 1997, all the eighth-grade students conducted conferences. Judy Feuge, a teacher at Floresville MS, reported that of the 250-plus eighth graders, all but 20 had a parent attend, and those without a parent had a conference with an adult guest. She said that, "Teachers were impressed, and students were amazed that their parents could come up to school without a teacher griping about them. It was fun to watch the students take control. Even our superintendent conferenced with a student!" (personal communication, April 17, 1997).

One remarkable result of the success of the first summer academy was that the summer school session in June 1997 did not have enough students to qualify for full funding from the state of Texas. The learning that students gained the first summer, when more than 100 fifth through eighth graders were required to attend, carried them successfully through the following year so that only 53 students needed summer school the following year. The overall retention rate at the school has been steadily dropping since the implementation of portfolios and conferencing in the summer of 1996 (see Figures 6.3 and 6.4), and Floresville's students have shown steadily increasing scores on the Texas Academic Achievement Skills tests (see Figure 6.5). Once again, results demonstrate the value of these two strategies in helping students learn more content.

Finally, portfolios and conferencing have become a regular part of the whole school's instruction and assessment so that during the 1997-98 school year, all the seventh- and eighth-grade students conducted two conferences with their parents or a guest. Dianne Porter, principal of Floresville Middle School, reports that due to the implementation of portfolios and student-led conferencing, the environment in her school has changed to one of collaboration and successful learning for all students. As Ms. Porter reflects, "There used to be a line of discipline problems outside my door every morning. Now, there are only a few in

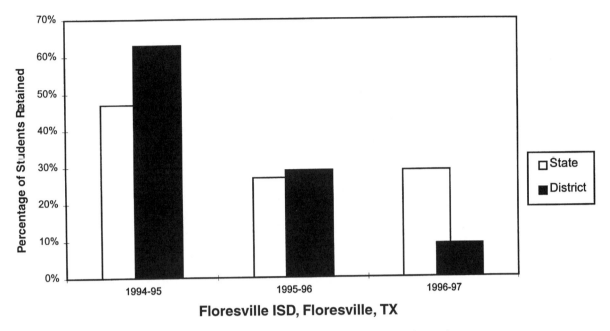

Figure 6.3. Effect of Using Portfolios and Student-Led Conferencing on Seventh-Grade Retention Rates

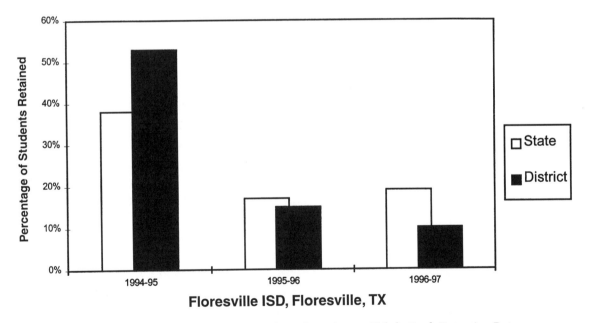

Figure 6.4. Effect of Using Portfolios and Student-Led Conferencing on Eighth-Grade Retention Rates

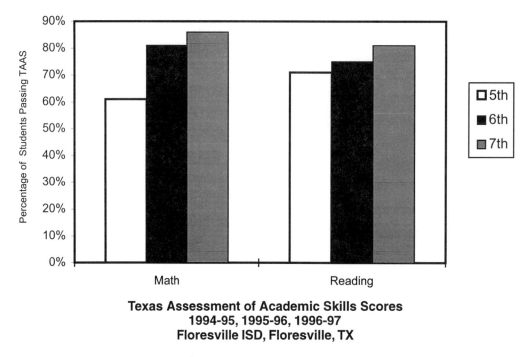

Figure 6.5. Three-Year Comparative Study (Same Students) Illustrating Positive Effects of Student-Led Conferencing on Standardized Test Scores

a day, and that is only the most obvious evidence that this school is a better place for all of us!" (personal communication, March 9, 1998).

Improvement in Elementary School

Can young students do this too? Jill Chapman, a kindergarten teacher in Broward County, Florida, says, "Yes, absolutely!" (personal communication, February 24, 1998). Even the youngest students can benefit from creating portfolios and conducting conferences. Ms. Chapman's proof comes from parents and students, and she relates that

> parents wrote letters back after the first conference saying that they never knew how much a kindergarten child could know. Their child took complete ownership, stayed on task, and had the confidence to demonstrate a high level of professionalism. At the second student-led conference, parents stated that their children were able to explain, define, and describe the process of how they learned and what they had learned over a period of time. (personal communication, February 24, 1998)

Another measure of the success and value of these strategies for young students is the fact that since Ms. Chapman began having her students do conferences, the entire faculty of Saw Grass elementary in Ft. Lauderdale, Florida, has begun to do the same. One of her colleagues reports that student-led conferencing shows a student's individual voice. She says that "It gives them a confidence level. It gives them an opportunity to shine. My second graders take 40 minutes for their conferences. They are very thorough. They show a lot of process (reading, writing, problem-solving, etc.) and how things work. The conference is meaningful and authentic" (J. Chapman, personal communication, February 24, 1998).

The reflections from Susan Barnett's first-grade parents in Boone, North Carolina, are similar to the responses in Broward County. Linda Hollar, a parent and high school teacher, writes that the student-led conferencing and portfolios helped her son

> learn verbal and organizational skills. The most beneficial of these skills is the self-confidence he has developed. If this type (of) instruction is used in the elementary grades, I can envision high school students who will be better all-round people because of the self-esteem this process develops. (personal communication, March 30, 1993).

Another set of parents, Mark and Carolyn Flahart, write that when their daughter

> started first grade this year, she was backward and shy, but now has blossomed into an outgoing and confident student who is very excited about learning. The idea of the kids holding their own conferences is wonderful! It really gives the children the confidence that they really can do anything they set out to do. (personal communication, April 2, 1993)

Other schools have seen equally remarkable successes in student learning and parent involvement. The statistics on improved student behavior, better performance on coursework, rising scores on standardized tests, and increased parent involvement, as well as the anecdotal evidence in written reflections and comments from teachers, students, and parents, offer proof of the power of these strategies to enhance the educational experience for all.

Conclusions

In any effort to change long-standing practice in schools, it is important that teachers have the process they will need. We also know, however, that the process needs to be flexible enough to adapt to the particular situations and talents of the teachers involved. We hope that we have given the essence of the process of using showcase portfolios in student-led conferences in a clear enough manner that a teacher can use this book as a recipe to implement the two strategies successfully.

We have also found that it is crucial for the teachers who are beginning this process to understand the theoretical basis for the strategies to be successful at adapting them to their own classrooms because things will not always go smoothly. When the students are not "getting it," the parents are not seeing the value of coming to school to look at portfolios, or the administration is not being completely supportive, teachers must believe in what they are doing to figure out how to get the results they want and to persevere. As Bobby Ann Starnes (1998) writes, new implementations of an innovative practice should look the same as the model but different because each teacher must live through the struggles necessary to own the new idea. Therefore, innovators must "be rigorous in uncovering, clarifying, and articulating an innovation's essential elements" (p. 40) without simplifying the method so much that it becomes empty parroting of the original idea. We hope that we have given the crucial pieces of the process but not made the recipe so easy that the cook no longer has to think! Our greatest desire is that readers can adapt student-led conferencing and showcase portfolios to their particular classrooms, schools, and communities. These two practices changed our classrooms for the better and are doing the same in a wide variety of classrooms and schools where they are being used. It is possible to motivate students to learn more, to get parents more involved in their children's education, and to enjoy making it happen. The journey is well worth the effort! We agree with a fifth-grade expert who evaluated student-led conferencing by saying, "I would recommend it, and I'd say, 'Go for it!' " (Roberts, 1996).

Resource A

Sample Forms

Teacher's Process for Implementing Portfolios:

PLANNING PROCESS:
- Determine the portfolio's purpose.
- Determine the audience for the portfolio.
- Determine possible format and organization.
- Determine possible contents.
- Decide how to inform students, parents, colleagues, and administrators.
- Begin!

IMPLEMENTATION WITH STUDENTS:
- Explain portfolio and its uses.
- Set quality standards - help students build habits for quality work.
- Teach organizational methods.
- Set aside time for students to collect/save materials, select appropriate pieces, assemble portfolio, assess portfolios, and share with an audience.
- Evaluate portfolios.

GETTING iT TOGETHER!!

THE STUDENT'S PROCESS FOR PORTFOLIOS:

- Save assignments and other evidence of learning.
- Select pieces for portfolio.
- Write required commentaries.
- Organize materials.
- Construct portfolio.
- Self-assess using portfolio rubric.
- Do Peer assessment for others as your portfolio is peer-assessed with rubric.
- Make any needed corrections, upgrades.
- Prepare for a conference to share portfolios.
- Share with outside audience.
- Turn in to be evaluated.

Dear Teacher,

Please take my picture when:

_____ I am reading alone

_____ I am working in a group

_____ I am presenting to the class

_____ I am taking a test

_____ I am reading aloud

_____ I am playing music

_____ I am creating art

_____ I am conferencing with my parents

_____ I am writing

_____ I am at P.E.

_____ I am enjoying learning

_____ I am thinking

_____ I am helping someone else learn

Place Photo Here

Name_____   Date _____

This picture shows me _____

_____

I wanted this picture in my portfolio
because_____

_____

_____

by:_____

This year I have learned to _____

_____

_____

_____.

I am really good at _____ because _____

_____

_____

_____.

This year I think _____ was hard because

_____

_____

_____.

The best part about school is when I _____

_____

_____

_____.

I am still learning many things. Next year I would like to learn about

_____

_____

_____

_____.

My Résumé

Name: _____

Address: _____

_____

Telephone #: _____

Birthday: _____

Education: _____

_____

_____

Work Experience: _____

_____

_____

Interests: _____

_____

Something Special About Me: _____

_____

References: _____

WEEKLY REFLECTION

Directions: As a successful learner, you are to think about the strategies, processes, activities, and interesting things you have learned this week in class. List your ideas on the planner below, share your planner with three other people and add any new ideas to your planner. Once you have organized your ideas on your planner, select 3 to 4 ideas that are most significant to you. Use these ideas to write a weekly letter to your parents telling them about what you have learned this week in school.

Math	Writing	Reading

Social Studies	Science	Specials or Up Coming Events

Benson and Barnett, *Student-Led Conferencing Using Showcase Portfolios.* Copyright 1999, Corwin Press, Inc.

Two Stars and a Wish

Worth a star.......

1

2

To improve, I wish......

My Tool Box

Have students write strategies
they use in certain content
areas like reading and math.

Guide for First Portfolio Evaluation

Your portfolio is due in two weeks. This portfolio should reflect your learning and development as a student during this marking period. Following is a statement of the minimum requirements for this portfolio. You may add more than what is listed here, but you must include all that is listed in order to have a complete portfolio. Before you turn in your portfolio, you should self-assess it, checking the appropriate boxes, and sign the guide sheet. You should also get a fellow student to assess it using the guide and signing it to indicate that the portfolio is ready to be evaluated.

SELF	BASELINE CONTENTS	PEER
	A title page with your name, a title for your portfolio, the date, and an appropriate quote with the source identified.	
	A "Preface" introducing yourself and stating your analysis of your goals for this course.	
	A Table of Contents listing the artifacts and commentaries in order. Page numbers are optional.	
	Three of the major writing assignments from this semester. These should have been revised to meet *Excellent* or *Acceptable* standards stated on the appropriate rubrics. Each writing assignment should have a **Commentary following it** which states what the original assignment was, why you selected this particular piece for your portfolio, and what this piece illustrates about your writing process, your improvement, and/or your learning/skill at this point.	

	One test from this marking period. This piece should have a **Commentary** which explains the test, discusses your performance on the test, and makes any necessary corrections to the test.	
	Three daily assignments [homework or class work] which show your learning and improvement. These should have a **Commentary** which discusses what the original assignments were, why you chose these three samples, and what they show about your learning and/or improvement.	
	OPTIONAL: You may also include one piece of your work which you feel proud of or which you feel shows improvement. This could come from another class and should have a **Commentary** which discusses what the sample is, why you chose it, and what it shows about you.	

Assess your portfolio using this guide then sign below to indicate that it is complete and ready to be peer-assessed.

_____

Signature of Peer Editor should follow, indicating that this portfolio is complete, meets course standards, and is ready to be turned in for evaluation.

_____

Once the rubric is signed, place it in the front of your portfolio. Put your Works in Progress Folder in the back of your portfolio and turn it in.

Date_____

Dear Parents and Guests,

On _____, your child will hold a student-led conference. You will be receiving a personal invitation from your child, scheduling the time and date. The purposes of the conferences for students are to:

- share their portfolios of quality work,
- practice communication skills,
- report on their school progress,
- practice organizational skills,
- assess their work honestly, and
- become accountable for their work and behavior.

This is an opportunity for you, as a parent, to show a positive interest in your child's progress, accept his or her assessment of the work and accomplishments as well as show your support and encouragement for his or her class work.

I will be in the room during the conferences should any clarification be necessary. There will be other opportunities for you to meet with me if either of us feels it necessary.

I look forward to seeing all of you on conference day.

Sincerely,

Benson and Barnett, *Student-Led Conferencing Using Showcase Portfolios.* Copyright 1999, Corwin Press, Inc.

An Important Message From Your Child's Teacher

Dear Parents,

Our philosophy of education focuses on teaching that is highly interactive, engaging students in making sense of ideas and applying what they learn to help them think critically, problem solve, and become self-directed learners. One way in which we hope to accomplish this is through Student-Led Conferencing.

Our students have spent a considerable amount of time and effort in preparing and designing an end-of-the-grading period conference. During this conference each child will share a portfolio of his/her personal best work documenting his/her progress in class. As your child shares his/her portfolio, we ask you to look for opportunities to make encouraging comments, help your child set goals and make a plan to reach these goals.

We appreciate your support and interest in your child's education. Please call if you have any questions or concerns.

Sincerely,

Teacher   **RSVP**

Student

Parent

Conference Date_____ Time_____

Please fill in this Conference form and return by_____

_____Yes, I would love to attend the conference my child is leading.

_____No, I am unable to attend, but would love to reschedule.

Comments:_____

_____

Benson and Barnett, *Student-Led Conferencing Using Showcase Portfolios.* Copyright 1999, Corwin Press, Inc.

Date_____

Dear _____,

You are invited to take part in a conference about my progress in my

_____ _____(subject)class. I will be conducting the conference and sharing

with you samples of my work in my portfolio. The reasons for this conference

are for you to see what I have been doing, see what I might need help on, and

celebrate my best work with me. I hope you will be able to attend the

conference. The conferences will be held on _____(date) in the

_____ from _____ to _____(time). I look

forward to talking with you at this time.

Sincerely,

RSVP: I will be able to attend our conference on _____(date).

OR

I will not be able to attend at the scheduled time, but would like to reschedule

the conference before or after school on _____(date).

Please indicate the time which you would like: _____.

Parent/Guest Signature:

_____

Date_____

Dear _____,

I am very _____ **about my conference that I will be**

leading on _____(day), _____(date),

at _____(time) in room _____. **I am**

looking forward to sharing.

_____

_____

_____

Having you at my conference is very important to me!

Please fill out the attached R.S.V.P. form and return it by _____ **(day),**

_____**(date). I know that sharing my progress with you is going to**

be

_____

_____

Love,

WELCOME TO OUR FIRST STUDENT-LED CONFERENCE

Dear Parents,

The students have worked very hard to prepare for this day. Your child will be sharing his/her portfolio with you. The work samples in the portfolio represent all areas of the curriculum and incorporate many skills. I ask that you praise your child because every child has made progress and has had accomplishments.

As your child shares the portfolio, you might want to ask the following questions:

"Tell me about this piece or assignment?"

"What did you have to do in the assignment?"

"What skills did you have to use?"

"What do you think you did well?"

"If you had to do this assignment again, what would you do to improve it?"

Following the conference, I would like <u>all</u> parents or guests to write a letter to the child commenting on the portfolio and the child's performance during the student-led conference. You may want to include some of the parent reflection ideas in your letter. Please return or mail your letter to school within the next week so that I can place the letter into your child's portfolio. The children will love to hear your reactions to their conferences. The school address is:

                   _____ (child's name)

c/o   _____ (teacher's name)

                   _____ (school address)

                   _____

                   _____

Thank you for your support.

                                                      Sincerely,

Benson and Barnett, *Student-Led Conferencing Using Showcase Portfolios.* Copyright 1999, Corwin Press, Inc.

Post Conference Parent Reflections

Dear Parents and Guests,

Please write a letter to your child reflecting on his/her performance during the student-led conference. Some items for discussion that you may want to use in your letter are listed below. Please return or mail your letter to school within the next week. Your letter will become part of your child's portfolio. Thank you again for choosing to take an active role in your child's education. Your participation reinforces to the student that his/her education and work are are important not only to you, but to his/her future.

Ideas for discussion in the letter:

- "I felt proud because…."
- "Keep up the good work on…."
- "I know that sometimes you have difficulty …. but…."
- "I am glad to see that you are taking an active role in your education by…."
- "I am glad to see that you are making an extra effort in…."
- "Some ways I can help you are…."
- "I enjoyed your conference because…."
- "Next time you may want to…."

Sincerely,

Benson and Barnett, *Student-Led Conferencing Using Showcase Portfolios*. Copyright 1999, Corwin Press, Inc.

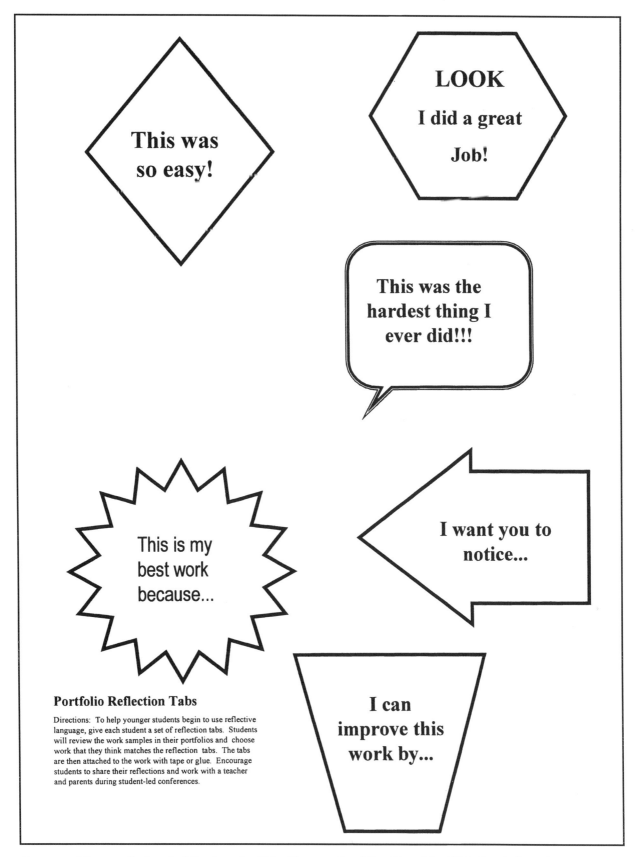

This was so easy!

LOOK

I did a great Job!

This was the hardest thing I ever did!!!

This is my best work because...

I want you to notice...

I can improve this work by...

Portfolio Reflection Tabs

Directions: To help younger students begin to use reflective language, give each student a set of reflection tabs. Students will review the work samples in their portfolios and choose work that they think matches the reflection tabs. The tabs are then attached to the work with tape or glue. Encourage students to share their reflections and work with a teacher and parents during student-led conferences.

Writing Reflection

As you think about yourself as a writer, answer the following questions:

1. You have worked hard as a writer these nine weeks. As you look over your work, what are two things you would want someone to notice about you as a writer?

2. You have completed many types of writing these nine weeks, what type of writing do you like the best?

3. How can what you have learned in writing help you away from school?

4. What do you find most difficult in writing? How can I help you?

MATH REFLECTION

As you think about yourself as a mathematician, answer the
following questions:

1. You have worked hard these nine weeks in math. As you look
   back over your work, what are two things you would want
   someone to notice about you as a math student?

2. What strategies have you learned these nine weeks in math?

3. How can you use what you have learned in math in the real
   world?

4. What do you find most difficult in math? What can I do to
   help you?

Benson and Barnett, *Student-Led Conferencing Using Showcase Portfolios.* Copyright 1999, Corwin Press, Inc.

READING REFLECTION

As you think of yourself as a reader, answer the following questions:

You have read several books these nine weeks. Which was your favorite book? Why?

How have you improved as a reader these nine weeks?

What are your goals for the next nine weeks?

What can I do to help you become a better reader?

BEST WORK

This is my favorite piece of work. I picked it for the following reasons:

1.

_____

_____

_____

2.

_____

_____

_____

3.

_____

_____

_____

Please write me a positive comment about my favorite piece of work:

_____

_____

_____

Commentary Form

The original assignment for this work was...

I selected this piece for my portfolio because...

What it shows about my learning is...

Reflecting on my work:

Portfolio Entry #:   Date:

Title/Type of Assignment:

This is what I learned:

I selected this for my portfolio because:

I want you to notice:

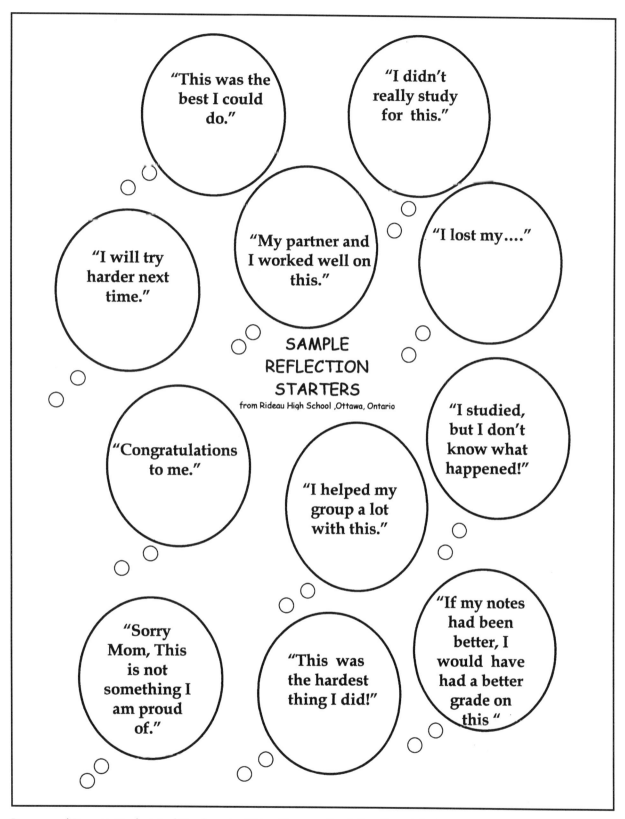

Benson and Barnett, *Student-Led Conferencing Using Showcase Portfolios.* Copyright 1999, Corwin Press, Inc.

Questions That Promote Student Self-Reflection

1. What makes this your best piece?

2. How did you go about writing/solving it?

3. What problems did you have? How did you solve them?

4. What makes this your most effective piece?

5. What goals did you set for yourself?
   How well did you accomplish them?

6. Why did you select this piece?

7. If you could go back and work some more on this piece, what would you do?

8. What was particularly important to you as you worked on the piece?

9. What do you want me to look for when I evaluate this work?

10. How does this relate to what you have learned before?

11. What grade would you put on this paper? Why?

12. Of the work we've done recently, I feel most confident about... .

13. I still don't understand... .

14. I (didn't) enjoy _____ because... .

15. I find _____ is most challenging because... .

Portfolio Entry # _____

Date:_____
Title:_____

This is what I have learned_____
_____
_____
_____
_____
_____ .

I selected this for my portfolio because_____
_____
_____
_____
_____ .

I want you to notice_____
_____
_____
_____
_____ .

Benson and Barnett, *Student-Led Conferencing Using Showcase Portfolios.* Copyright 1999, Corwin Press, Inc.

PORTFOLIO ENTRY COVER SHEET

1. Explain the assignment in detail.

2. What of importance did you learn from the assignment? *(skills, strategies, ideas, concepts, group processing, etc.)*

3. How does this portfolio entry relate to the "real world"? What did you learn/use that will help you outside the classroom?

4. In this assignment, what do you particularly want others to notice?

5. What would you improve if you could do this over again?

Portfolio Visits

Name	Date	Comments
1.		
2.		
3.		
4.		
5.		
6.		
7.		
8.		
9.		
10.		

Benson and Barnett, *Student-Led Conferencing Using Showcase Portfolios.* Copyright 1999, Corwin Press, Inc.

Welcome to my world!

*I want you to know
     that I love it when......*

In school I get excited about.......

My favorite activity is..........

I am best at.......

I need to improve.........

You can help me by ....

Getting Ready for My Conference

1. What did I learn this quarter?

2. What have I done really well?

3. What do I need to do better?

4. Who can help me improve?

5. What is my goal for next quarter?

6. What strategies
   can I use?

Student-Led Conferencing Sign-Up Sheet

Student	Parents/Guests	Date
1		
2		
3		
4		
5		
6		
7		
8		
9		
10		
11		
12		
13		
14		
15		
16		
17		
18		
19		
20		

Conference "Thank You Cards"

HEADING: Date

GREETING: Dear_____

BODY: Tell your guests that you want to thank
                 them for:

                1.Attending... .
                2.Listening to ... .
                3.Supporting... .
                4.Showing understanding and concern....
                5.Commenting on....

                                      CLOSING

                                    SIGNATURE

                                      Date_____

Dear _____,

      Thank you for coming to my conference on _____.

I really enjoyed showing you my portfolio. I appreciated it when

you_____.

The best part of the conference was when _____.

I hope you enjoyed it as much as I did.

                                    Love,

Post-Conference Student Reflection

Name: Date:

Things went smoothly during the conference because....

Things could have gone better if....

One thing I wish I would have shared, but forgot....

One thing I should have shared, but didn't....

I benefitted from this conference because....

Some ways my parents benefited from hearing my perspective and seeing my portfolio were....

TIME TO REFLECT

Please take a minute and reflect about your experience with student-led conferencing.
What went well...

How many of your parents attended...
Parent reactions...

Students reactions...

Things you would have done differently...

Please share any anecdotes, positive experiences, parent comments about student-led conferences...

[Be sure to save any copies of student prefaces, reflections, comments and any "good stuff" that parents, guests or kids said or did related to conferences.]

MEMO: Student-Led Conferencing Follow-Up
TO: All Classroom Teachers
FROM: The Principal

Congratulations on a wonderful turn out of parents last night at the student-led conferences. It was so exciting to see the smiling faces of students, parents, and teachers. It definitely was a win-win situation for all involved.

Even though conference night is over, it is still important that you personally contact any parents who were unable to attend their child's conference and make arrangements for them to come into school next week. If after several phone calls, you are still unable to arrange a conference for a student with his/her parents or another significant substitute, then let me know, and I will find someone to conference with that student.

We have the individual classroom percentages of students attending last night and plan to post them as soon as they are confirmed. Any additional conferences held next week will be included in your total classroom percentage. Wouldn't it be great if we had 100% parent participation?

Again thank you for all your hard work. Good Job!

Directions for a Commentary on a Professional Reading:

Read one article on reading, writing and/or math. Write a brief summary of the reading and your reaction to it. Also include a statement telling how you could adapt what you have learned to your own situation or classroom.

Sample Commentary:

Carbo, M. (1990, October). Igniting the literacy revolution through reading styles. Educational Leadership.

The article emphasizes the need to match instructional methods with students' reading styles in order to produce students who are capable readers. The author recommends five methods that could make a significant difference in the reading performance of students: identify students' reading styles; use reading methods and materials that match reading style strengths; demonstrate high expectations for students' achievement and high levels of respect for their different styles; use reading materials that reflect the students' interests; and remove stress from learning to read.

The author states that students associate reading with pain and that they will read only when the process becomes easy and pleasurable. I find this to be particularly true in regard to my own children. My oldest son did not became an accomplished reader until the summer between fifth and sixth grade. After he failed reading in fifth grade, I insisted that he read a book a week and write a book report. I did not care what he read or the length of the book report, just as long as he read. By the end of the summer, he had fallen in love with books and has since become a voracious reader. My other child, on the other hand, struggles with reading everyday. To him it is an incredibly difficult task. He knows he has trouble with reading and is embarrassed because of it. He spends a lot of time trying to cover up for his inability to read well.

After reading the article, I realized that I have already incorporated some of Ms. Carbo's recommendations into my own teaching. When I return to the classroom, I plan to use some form of reading styles inventory with my students. I have heard about the Carbo Method of teaching reading and would like to try it with my own students.

Resource B

A Word About Other Types of Portfolios

Process Portfolios

Process portfolios are intended to show a student's progress through a particular period of time or on a particular skill. In these portfolios, students collect all the work related to the specific concept or skill being demonstrated. For example, if the portfolio is to demonstrate progress in math, it might contain the first work on a concept, the homework with corrections, the test, perhaps a project or presentation on the concept, and the student's final discussion of the learning and progress accomplished. This type of portfolio might sound like the writing folders language arts teachers often keep to illustrate student writing progress, but without student reflection and goal setting, those writing folders are not true portfolios.

Ideas for a Process Portfolio

- Be sure to tell students to keep all steps and work of the process being documented.
- Teachers should model strategies for helping students keep and reflect on work samples over a period of time.
- Students should sum up the collected pieces by writing a discussion of the process they went through and what they learned by doing it.
- This portfolio might include poor student performances as well as better ones so that the progress can be seen in the contrast between the two types of work samples. Students should reflect on the poor samples to analyze what needs to be improved and set goals. They also need to reflect on the progress they see between the poor and the later, improved samples.

These portfolios are collected samples of work relating to a particular class or school project. A research paper, if it includes the student's reflection on the work, can be a special project portfolio. For example Ron Wilson, a math teacher in Woodward, Oklahoma, had his ninth-grade algebra class create special project portfolios at the end of the year. As a means of reviewing for the state end-of-course test in algebra, the students worked in pairs and created *Cliff's Notes for Algebra I.* Their special project portfolios included the major concepts from the year's course, sample student-made problems and tests with correction sheets, and reflections on the year's work and their own progress. These portfolios were so successful that the students wanted them back to sell to the next class taking the course! Some examples of special projects portfolios for young students might be a colors unit for kindergartners, a unit on dinosaurs for second graders, or a unit focusing on poetry and the creation of a poetry book for sixth graders. These special portfolios may contain graphs and problem solving in math, timelines, notes, writing, artwork, student research, group work, quizzes, reflections, and commentaries.

A special project portfolio can be a good way to begin using portfolios because it offers students and the teacher the experience of creating a portfolio without a long-term commitment. Doing this type of portfolio can also assist a teacher in developing the processes that could be used later with a showcase portfolio of a grading period or a year's work. If the reflection on the work in the project is included in the student's presentation of the process and results of the project, the piece becomes a portfolio.

Special Project Portfolios

Ideas for a Special Project Portfolio

- Pick a project for the portfolio that will be long-term, will require complex thinking, and will offer some student choice in subject or means of demonstrating the learning.
- Allow students to work in pairs or small teams; this can be useful in helping students produce quality work.
- Students need to keep samples of their work and reflections throughout the project. Again, the teacher may need to model ways to do this.
- Something like a science fair project can be the subject of a special project portfolio. Obviously, the finished, physical project may be impossible to put in a portfolio, but photographs, a written report of the project, a discussion of the process the student went through to complete the project, and any evaluation of the project, including prizes or recognition, can be placed in the portfolio along with student reflections about the learning.

- Students should sum up the collected work in the portfolio by writing (dictating for younger students) a discussion of the process they went through, what they learned, and what they gained from it. The sophistication of the writing naturally depends on the ability and age of the student.

Pass-Along Portfolios

Schoolwide pass-along portfolios are being used in some school systems to follow student progress as students advance from one grade level to the next. These portfolios are designed to demonstrate curriculum alignment and document specific skill requirements, teacher assessments, and other relevant student information. Often, these progressive portfolios (particularly in the earlier grades) are collections of student work samples selected by the teacher to convey student information to the teacher at the next grade level, but not true portfolios with student input and reflection. A good pass-along portfolio can give teachers information to help them prepare to meet the learning needs of the students entering their classrooms. In middle and high school, pass-along portfolios tend to be done in selected content areas. For example, many language arts departments collect and pass along samples of student writing. These collections might even be part of a statewide initiative, as in Kentucky's math and language arts portfolios.

Ideas for Pass-Along Portfolios

- Developing pass-along portfolios should begin with cross-grade-level teacher discussions concerning the format and specific contents of the portfolio and methods of gathering and organizing student work.
- Specific contents of pass-along portfolios may include the following: work samples that show student progress over time, state and local assessments, state and local benchmarks, report cards or progress reports, state and local writing test information, content-concept tests, projects, learning logs, student self-assessments, writing samples, interest inventories, self-portraits, parent conference summaries, student conference summaries, anecdotal notes, observation notes, interview notes, audio- and videotapes, artwork, and checklists.
- Even though the contents may be specified by the school or system, students still need to have a say in what goes into their portfolios.
- If students are required to have a pass-along portfolio, the teachers or the school should use them as part of the assessment and instructional processes. Many times such documents are passed

along but never used, making the creation of the document mean-
ingless to students.

- We strongly believe that students should own their own portfolio
and recommend that if a system has a required pass-along portfolio, students have a showcase portfolio that they will take home at
the end of the year. This showcase portfolio might include many
of the same artifacts as the system's pass-along portfolio, but if the
students do not have one of their own, they will not be as motivated
to do well because the portfolio is not theirs. It belongs to the
school and is probably seen as just another type of test.

Passport portfolios are required by a school or system as part of the
certification for a student to move on to another grade level or to
graduate from the system. Passport portfolios are especially common in
schools that require senior projects or graduation by exhibition. Some
samples of this kind of portfolio are the senior project portfolios being
used in Oregon and the portfolios created by students at Central Park
East Secondary School in New York City. ACT, the national testing service
for college admissions, has created a portfolio assessment system called
PASSPORT. In language arts, science, and mathematics, 9th- through
12th-grade students create portfolios encompassing a prescribed number
of work samples and cover letters to explain their entries. J. L. Happel
(1997), assessment specialist for ACT, states that this system is "designed
to promote improvement of student performance and to document that
improvement over time. PASSPORT involves students in setting goals,
defining projects, and assessing their progress." Presumably, the portfolios developed in the ACT PASSPORT program would also be used to
help certify student learning and achievement to colleges and universities.

Passport Portfolios

Ideas for Passport Portfolios

- As with pass-along portfolios, if the passport portfolio is collected
according to exact system requirements and the teacher's selection
of pieces, students should have a personal portfolio as well. The
required pieces for the system's portfolio can be taken or copied
from originals in the student's portfolio. Student ownership in the
process is important and sometimes is missing if the portfolio is so
prescribed that it really belongs to the school, not the student.
- If a system is designing a passport portfolio, it is crucial that student
reflection on the work, learning, and improvement be included in
the entries.
- These portfolios should be tied directly to required elements of the
content students should know and competencies they should have
developed by the specific grade level using the portfolios. What-

ever goes in them should demonstrate the student's progress towared national, state, and local standards.

Teachers'
Professional
Portfolios

Professional portfolios for teachers are becoming one of the tools used by educational institutions to certify new teachers, hire staff, and evaluate teaching performance of existing staff. They offer teachers a golden opportunity to have input into the evaluation process. As K. Wolf (1996) states, "When carefully conceived, portfolios can significantly advance a teacher's professional growth. They can also ensure that evidence of exemplary teaching doesn't vanish without a trace" (p. 34). They are necessary for teachers who are having their students create showcase portfolios. If a teacher has not created a portfolio, how can that teacher possibly know the ups and downs of the process well enough to help students through it? By doing his or her own portfolio, a teacher is also modeling the skills the students will need. As L. Van Wagenen and K. M. Hibbard (1998) write, "A teacher's portfolio enables us to do exactly what we ask our students to do: self-assess, self-evaluate, and self-regulate" (p. 29).

Just as with student portfolios, the purpose the teacher has for the portfolio will determine how the portfolio is organized and what goes into the collection. If a system has specific areas of expertise expected of teachers, and a teacher wishes to use his or her portfolio as documentation for evaluation, the portfolio should be organized by those required areas. For example, Texas has instituted a new evaluation system for teachers that is organized by eight domains. A teacher in Texas who wants to use a portfolio to document professional competence could use those domains to organize a professional portfolio, putting artifacts appropriate to each domain in one of eight labeled sections. The commentaries accompanying artifacts would discuss how particular samples reflect the teacher's competence in that domain. Without the commentaries, the artifacts are merely a scrapbook that few people will understand.

If a teacher is using the portfolio to apply for a job or a change in position within a system, however, the portfolio might be organized according to the professional duties that teacher fulfills. The collection might be organized chronologically showing the teacher's year, or by courses the teacher teaches and professional activities in which the teacher participates.

When the teacher's portfolio is intended as a model for student portfolios or as a personal collection to demonstrate professional growth, it might be organized in many other ways. For example, for a model portfolio, the teacher could follow the organization that the students will follow, including the types of artifacts students will have. In the case of a professional growth portfolio, the collection could be organized to show the process of investigating a particular focus question throughout the year. This type of portfolio may include things that worked well in class and things that need improvement. For items that show weaknesses or problems, the teacher would then have reflections and methods that he or she used to improve the situations.

Finally, a professional portfolio can be used for the purpose of holding teachers accountable for implementing major classroom instructional and assessment strategies being explored in districtwide staff development or school improvement programs. The Uvalde School District in south Texas has been involved in a multiyear effort to improve student performance and preparation for the 21st century. Teachers who go through training are expected to create portfolios demonstrating their learning, use of new strategies, and achievement of expectations that the district has for participants. These portfolios are organized according to the expectations that teachers become information accessors, constructive thinkers, quality producers, effective communicators, and self-reflective learners.

In another example of portfolios for accountability, teachers in a low-performing elementary school in North Carolina are required to create portfolios organized around the staff development they are receiving and how they are implementing strategies, improving their own professional knowledge, and improving student learning in their classrooms. One of the ways they are increasing their professional knowledge base in reading, writing, and math is by doing focused professional reading; therefore, one type of artifact they have in their portfolios is commentaries they write on articles they have read (see p. 139 in Resource A).

Professional teacher portfolios may contain many types of artifacts and be organized in various ways, but they must have the reflective commentaries so they are "more than a miscellaneous collection of artifacts or an extended list of professional activities" (Wolf, 1996, p. 34). Numerous publications offer ideas for and validation of portfolios for teachers who are seeking to improve their teaching, and we recommend that teachers investigate available resources as they decide to create their own portfolios.

Possible Contents for Professional Portfolios

- A preface introducing yourself and stating professional mission and goals for the year
- Current resume
- Sample integrated unit of instruction with sample lesson plans, commentaries, and student work
- Sample classroom assessment strategies and tests
- Evidence of using strategies and instructional practices learned in staff development and commentaries discussing how the implementation worked in the classroom

- Commentaries on professional reading relating to current issues, research, and classroom practice (see p. 139 in Resource A)
- Year-long instructional plans and timelines
- Commentaries on lessons you felt were particularly successful with students
- Newspaper articles concerning student or teacher success
- Newly developed classroom materials
- Documentation of communications with parents
- Evidence of collaborative work with colleagues
- For new teachers, college transcripts and professional test scores
- Copy of a professional evaluation
- Awards and letters of commendation or recommendation
- Published works
- Videotaped lessons
- Photographs of class activities with commentaries
- Documentation of presentations in workshops, professional meetings, conventions, and school board meetings
- Professional activities such as membership in professional organizations, active participation on school committees, and membership on local or state commissions involved in school improvement
- Evidence of growth as a teacher; reflections on a lesson(s) that did not work and what you did to improve it
- Analysis of classroom management techniques
- Statements of risk taking and results
- Evidence of movement toward and alignment with district's improvement plans and state or national content standards
- Continuous improvement plan with progress updates
- Sample reflections from a teacher's journal
- Focus question(s) for investigation, progress, and results of action research, conclusions, and plans for future action
- Epilogue to sum up your use of new knowledge, share plans for the future, explain progress toward goals stated in the preface, and offer a final reflection on the year

References

Aguayo, R. (1990). *Dr. Deming*. New York: Simon & Schuster.

Burke, K. (1993). *The mindful school: How to assess authentic learning*. Palatine, IL: IRI/Skylight.

California Department of Education. (1996). *Golden State Exam Science portfolio guide*. Sacramento, CA: Author.

Central Park East Secondary School. (1991). *Central Park East Secondary School graduation requirements*. New York: Author.

Collins. A., & Dana, T. M. (1993, November). Using portfolios with middle grades students. *Middle School Journal*, pp. 14-19.

Donahue, F., Marmo, D., & Soto, G. (1994). Excellence in education looks like Southridge Middle School! *The High Success Connection, 3*(4), 1-3.

Floresville Achievement Academy graduates first class. (1996, July 24). *Chronicle Journal*.

Grissom, J. (1997). *Nomination packet for governor's 1997-1998 programs of excellence in education*. Submitted to North Carolina Department of Public Instruction.

Guidance Centre. (1994). *Employability skills portfolio*. Toronto: Ontario Institute for Studies in Education.

Haggard, G. (1998, Spring). Portfolios: One district's journey. *Reading Recovery Council Connections*, 15-16.

Hamm, M. E., & Adams, D. M. (1992, February). Portfolio assessment and social studies: Collecting, selecting, and reflecting on what is significant. *Social Education*, 103-105.

Happel, J. (1997). Letter accompanying *Passport* promotional material. ACT Test Development, Iowa City.

IRA/NCTE Joint Task Force on Assessment. (1994). *Standards for the assessment of reading and writing*. Urbana, IL: International Reading Association and National Council of Teachers of English.

Knight, P. (1992). How I use portfolios in mathematics. *Educational Leadership, 49*(8), 71-72.

Lincoln County School of Technology. (1996). *Employment portfolio*. Lincoln, NC: Author.

McTighe, J. (1997). What happens between assessments? *Educational Leadership, 54*(4), 6-12.

Merina, A. (1993). When bad things happen to good ideas. *NEA Today, 12*, 4-5.

Newmann, F. M., & Wehlage, G. C. (1993). Five standards of authentic instruction. *Educational Leadership, 50*(7), 8-12.

Niguidula, D. (1997). Picturing performance with digital portfolios. *Educational Leadership, 55*(3), 26-29.

North Carolina Department of Public Instruction. (Producer). (1992). *Portfolios: Not just for artists anymore* [Videotape]. Raleigh: Author.

Rideau High School's Portfolio Committee. (1997). *Portfolios at Rideau High School: Teacher's handbook.* Ottawa, Ontario: Author.

Roberts, N. (Ed.). (1996). *Student-led conferences survey: A compilation of student responses.* Ottawa, Ontario: Crichton Alternative Community Public School.

Schunk, D. (1990). Goal setting and self-efficacy during self-regulated learning. *Educational Psychologist, 25*(1), 71-86.

Seidel, S., & Walters, J. (1992). *The design of portfolios for authentic assessment, project zero.* Boston: Harvard Graduate School of Education.

Smith, T. K. (1997). Authentic assessment: Using a portfolio card in physical education. *JOPERD, 68*(4), 46-52.

Spady, W. (1994, July). *Reaching new heights in learning by transforming our paradigm of education.* Speech at opening general session of High Success Network Conference, Vail, CO.

Starnes, B. A. (1998). On cargo cults and educational innovation. *Education Week, 27*(34), 38, 40.

Van Wagenen, L., & Hibbard, K. M. (1998). Building teacher portfolios. *Educational Leadership, 55*(5), 26-29.

Wesley, N. (1993, April). College placement portfolios help high schools teach writing. *Council Chronicles,* p. 7.

Willis, S. (1990, Fall). Using technology to transform physical education. *ASCD Curriculum Update, 5.*

Willis, S. (1994). Educational leaders learn by doing. *ASCD Update, 36*(1), 1, 3, 8.

Wolf, K. (1996). Developing an effective teaching portfolio. *Educational Leadership, 53*(6), 34-37.